I Left My Sole in Vermont

A Walker's Journey and Guide
Through Central Vermont Back Roads

Nicole Grubman

I Left My Sole in Vermont

Nicole Grubman

A Walker's Journey and Guide Through Central Vermont Back Roads

Published by **RED BARN BOOKS** *of vermont*   Red Barn Books of Vermont
An imprint of Wind Ridge Books
Shelburne, Vermont 05482

I Left My Sole in Vermont
A Walker's Journey and Guide Through Central Vermont Back Roads

Copyright 2013 by Nicole Grubman

Published by Red Barn Books of Vermont
P.O. Box 636
Shelburne, Vermont 05482

ISBN: 978-1-935922-30-8

We should go forth on the shortest walk, perchance, in the spirit of undying adventure, never to return—prepared to send back our embalmed hearts only as relics to our desolate kingdoms. If you are ready to leave father and mother, and brother and sister, and wife and child and friends, and never see them again—if you have paid your debts, and made your will, and settled all your affairs, and are a free man—then you are ready for a walk.

— Henry David Thoreau

"It's a dangerous business, Frodo, going out your door. You step onto the road, and if you don't find your feet, there's no knowing where you might be swept off to."

— J.R.R Tolkein, The Lord of the Rings

Washington County Walks

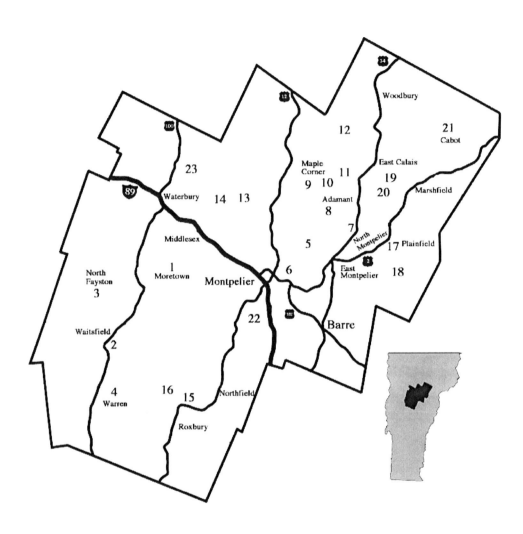

Contents

Foreword

"Here I am once again for the first time." She says it's her mantra, though I've only actually heard her say it out loud once. But it is true; that's her way of being in the world: a state of perpetual returning, continually arriving back at the starting point to find herself and everything exactly as she left it—completely different.

Of course, all such philosophical musings are the furthest thing from my mind at moments like this. "How does she move like that?" is more in line with my actual thoughts as I watch her black Honda Shadow vanish around the next hairpin a quarter mile ahead of me. Not much of a mantra, it's a thought that has become familiar to me in the years that I've been spending time with Nicole.

Gasping for air as she scrambles up a rock fall thirty feet above my head, staring at the wake of her kayak as it cuts through the water on the far side of the island, praying that I don't twist an ankle or explode a knee by foolishly trying to keep up as she sprints down the mountain we have just spent the entire morning climbing. I am constantly asking myself that same question: "How does she move like that?"

At first, it used to annoy me. Now, I just accept it. It's like having a superhero or a ninja for a best friend. Moving through space is what she does, and trying to keep up is fun. And terrifying. Besides, I know she won't let me fall too far behind. I know she'll wait for me at the next stop sign, smile under those crazy motorcycle goggles she wears, and shout something encouraging over the roar of our idling bikes such as, "This next dirt road is a bit washed out; remember to lay off the front brake!" But still, how does she move like that? And how much farther to the start of the walk?

Ah, the walk! That's when everything will shift. We'll park our bikes and pass through the magic gate. The world will get quiet. My head will get quiet. The world of noise and movement and objectives will drop away, because that is another one of her mysterious talents: finding the magic gate.

I know it's corny, but that's how I think of it. How else to explain the shift that happens every time I follow her to one of her back-road walking loops? I can think of no other way to describe the passage into some parallel existence where the mind can relax because the dirt beneath your feet is willing to make all your decisions for you.

Believe me. Or don't. But only try it. Pick one of the walks in this book at random. Leave your phone. Clear your mind of thought and focus your intention. Or don't. It won't matter. The road will do all the work for you. The crunch of gravel under your boots, the naked trees and moss-covered stone walls, time measured out in footfalls and heartbeats. On the other side of the magic gate they have the power to carry you off. And bring you back.

"Here I am once again for the first time."

Try it. Trust me. You'll get it.

And, eventually, so will I. Somewhere beyond that next hairpin, the magic gate is waiting. Pass through it, and, I promise, before your engine has cooled off you'll find yourself someplace completely new, and reassuringly familiar.

There you'll be once again for the first time.

—*Mark Stein*

Preface

It was challenging to decide which loops to include in this book. I could have written a guidebook covering the entire state. Then I would not have to leave out some of my favorite walks up north in Lincoln and Huntington or down south in towns such as Stockbridge and Braintree. But I wanted to focus on roads that captured the essential character of this magnificent place—roads that are still actively used by the people who live and work here. After years of exploring, I feel called to share the journey that led me straight into the heart and soul of Vermont. It has been an extended expedition leading up past old farms and common areas perched high above village centers. It has been a personal passage along the meandering lanes where creative homesteads and junk metal sculptures lie hidden in shady hollows.

I decided to focus on Washington County. Located in Central Vermont, it is the only county other than Lamoille that does not border another state. Montpelier, the county seat, is also the state capital. No urban mecca, Montpelier lies quaint and cozy in the Winooski River Valley.

Other than the interstate, it is hard to find a road in Washington County that runs straight for more than a few miles. The villages and surrounding areas fit neatly into the topography, connected by curvy roads that follow the rolling, pastoral landscape. These are roads whose origins are the forgotten footfalls of people, for whom it made more sense to meander around—rather than break through.

It is easy to feel Central Vermont's authenticity but hard to define it. When I walk on the roads radiating from Montpelier an internal shift occurs. I lose my bearing and can't get a good sense of direction. Time slows down and then moves to the rhythm of my walking. The beautiful surroundings and friendly people provide a backdrop that encourages my soul to become more visible.

I can't quite put my finger on the magic of Washington County. Maybe it's the way the mountains flow seamlessly into the valley, how the wilderness and working landscape are so intertwined. Maybe it's because while the rest of the world moves so quickly, the people living on Central Vermont's back roads slow things down. Maybe it's because while the rest of the world builds more fast-food restaurants and big-box stores, people along Central Vermont's back roads grow their own food and live more simply. They host potlucks for new neighbors and come together for weekend pond hockey tournaments.

Whatever the reason, I think Washington County epitomizes everything Vermont was, is, and continues to become. The walks in this book make me feel grateful to call this sacred haven my home. While I want the places in this book to remain hidden, you deserve the opportunity to share the beauty of what I've found by wandering deep into the circular roads of Vermont's soulful center.

Acknowledgments

This book has been a labor of love and a process of discovery. I am grateful to all the wonderful people who helped make this dream become a reality.

Thank you, thank you, and thank you to:

My family, for inspiring me to find my own unique way and loving me for who I am and what I am becoming,

Nona Estrin, who was a mentor and inspiration through the initial phases of this extensive project,

David Coburn, head of the East Montpelier Historical Society, who graciously invited me to his old farmhouse and brought to life the stories of times past but not forgotten,

Jane Petrillo and Colin Byrne from the University of Vermont Art Department, who selflessly volunteered their time and talent to design all the walking maps,

Emily Mahon, my dear childhood friend, who created the cover design and assisted in touching up the photographs found throughout the book,

Mark Stein, for his tireless editing and for continually reminding me of the gentle yet sustaining power of love and true friendship, and

My friends, who kept me company during my back-road adventures. Through the rain, snow, mud, and cold you have all remained faithfully by my side, never doubting that we would always find our way back around.

PART 1:

Wonderings

Walking Tips for the Road

Good form for walking:
- Keep an open stance and a strong center.
- Extend long through the backs of the legs.
- Reach with the heel and ground down through the inner edge of the foot.
- Lift through the crown of the head and keep the shoulders relaxed.
- Engage the core by kissing the belly button up and in toward the spine.

Tips for hill walking:
- Keep the same pace but take smaller steps.
- Try not to get into the habit of placing your step on the balls of your feet, as this will make for sore calves.
- If you get tired, want to work your quadriceps, or take in the view behind you, experiment with walking backward (and being silly)!

Safety Tips:
- Walk facing traffic—This gives you the best chance to see approaching vehicles and take evasive action when needed.
- Be visible—Wear bright colors when walking in daytime. When walking at dawn or twilight, wear light-colored clothing or a reflective vest.
- Wear comfortable shoes and clothing—There is an expression in New England: "If you don't like the weather just wait a few minutes." Plan accordingly and dress in layers. Most of the walks go through shady areas or along ridgelines exposed to wind. Use common sense and make sure you have appropriate clothing for the season, good socks, and comfortable shoes with decent traction. If rain is predicted, bring a waterproof jacket.

- Bring a small snack and water—No matter how short the loop, it is always a good idea to bring water and some emergency food. An energy bar, apple, or trail mix are great walking snacks.
- Don't overburden yourself—The delight of walking lies in its simplicity. Don't weigh yourself down with excessive equipment or gear. You can bring a small journal or a camera to document your journey, but try to travel light so you can enjoy the buoyancy of an empty mind and the freedom of the open road.

Introduction:
The Original Walk—Mud City Loop

On Sunday mornings many things happen. I ponder my Monday adventure. I brainstorm. I pore over the classified section of the local newspaper, look at maps, or read the dictionary. One Sunday I was perusing the classified section of the Burlington Free Press over a delicious breakfast: steamed greens, a poached egg, and some well-toasted rye. Moving my coffee aside, I noticed a small advertisement; "Free, vintage women's wardrobe: Morrisville, VT." This ad changed my life.

Ten years ago I was in my strictly polyester phase and thought I had struck gold. I called the number and spoke with an elderly woman. She had a closet full of suits from her days as a Pan Am stewardess. This was back when airlines served meals on china and flying was reserved for the elite. We set a time to meet for the following Monday.

But I digress, just like my favorite roads. This is a book of digressions. It is a meander through secret places, like the adventure of walking a road where you can't see around the shadowed corner or up beyond the big maple. It will wander though the wonderings that happen when our feet, and our minds, forsake the direct route for the twisting, circuitous path. But, as usual, I get ahead of myself. That's why I walk: to give myself time to catch up.

So Monday arrived and I had to find this address in Morrisville on a road called Mud City Loop. Since I'm a bit of a Luddite, I prefer to find my way around using paper maps instead of the computer or a GPS. Referencing my trusted Vermont Gazetteer, I found the aptly named Mud City Loop. The road circles around the Lamoille County Nature Center, forming a circuit at the base of Sterling Ridge. I outlined the entire loop in yellow highlighter, wondering how the road would play out in real life. The loop was magical. The suits were fabulous. The lady became a fascinating friend.

Throughout the following ten years, I returned to Mud City Loop more times than I can count. It was the walk that inspired me to begin this journey. Mud City Loop reveals new treasures each time you walk it: secret swimming holes under high bridges, the sound of sap drip-ping into metal buckets, an unexpected autumnal snowstorm cascading over the ridge, a spontaneous romp across the tops of freshly bound hay bales, black-spotted calves suckling on cold fingers …

This is the way of the loop. It rescues from oblivion the moments our busy lives may otherwise obscure. Unassuming but arresting places of quiet beauty create the content of the journey. Free from the constant nagging question 'Where am I going?' the wanderer finds time outside the everyday grind of constant doing, time to access the open space that encourages the mind to empty.

End at the beginning, and in so doing learn how to arrive. Focus on the way your feet sound on gravel and dirt. Open your senses; enter gen-tly into the moment. Notice how the rhythm of your heartbeat matches the cadence of your footsteps. Become aware of how the flow of your thoughts, when you let them pass, matches the steady movement of your breath. Wander and wonder down the road.

Walking as Meditation: Opening into the Road

The goal of conscious walking is to increase awareness. It is an opportunity to fully encounter the internal and external landscape by becoming an interactive witness. You can allow your mind to wander or maintain focus on your senses. Notice how intentional movement transforms consciousness. Be curious about what is different when you arrive back to where you started.

The practice of walking gives the mind space to wonder. The only goal is to discover *your self* in connection with the moment. Since walking a loop is a process of discovering, whatever you find will become an object of fascination.

The Meditation of Walking

1. ### Observe the mind

   - Start by seeing what the mind wonders.
   - Recognize that during your walk you do not have to respond to your thoughts, your lists, or your fears.
   - Let your thoughts pass as gently as the scenery.
   - Notice the things you do that distract yourself from the experience of the road. At the beginning of walks I tend to fiddle with stuff. I might adjust my backpack, re-lace my shoes, take off my scarf, vigorously chew on my peppermint gum, or superfluously reference my map.
   - Witness.

2. ### Attend to breath

   - Be aware of breathing in and breathing out.
   - Breathe automatically and freely. Do not try to control your breath.
   - Feel air entering the mouth or nose, filling the lungs, and pushing out again.

- Discover whether you breathe through your belly, your diaphragm, or the upper part of your chest.
- Notice the way the rib cage expands outward on the inhalation and hugs back to center on the exhalation.

Quick exercise if the mind is too busy to focus on breath …

- If the mind cannot focus on the breath, push air out of the mouth as though you are blowing through an imaginary straw. Exhale forcefully but slowly. Empty your lungs completely.
- This exercise releases stress and helps the mind to clear. Imagine your exhalation as a dark cloud of thoughts and worry leaving your body.

3. Extend awareness to the physical sensation of walking

- Notice how the flow of breath interacts with the rhythm of your steps.
- Listen to the regular cadence of your feet making contact with the road.
- Focus on initiating your walk from your center (core) and then extending energy out and down through the legs.
- As your weight rolls forward from heel to toes, ground through your big toe.
- Keep your core engaged by pulling your belly button toward your spine.
- Extend upward through the crown of your head as you press downward through the bottoms of your feet. This creates length in your body to allow more room for breath to enter.
- Keep your shoulders relaxed and away from your neck.
- Allow your arms to hang loosely by your sides. Circle your wrists to release tension and send energy out through your fingertips.
- Try counting your steps as you walk. See how many you can count off before losing focus.

4. Use your senses to feel the moment

TOUCHING: Imagine breathing in and out through your skin and opening through your pores. Make a mental list of everything that you experience through touch.

Example:
- I feel cold wind blowing under my scarf.
- I feel warmth coming from the west as the sun sets.
- I feel fine dirt hit the top of my right hand after a car speeds by.
- I feel numbness in my left pinky toe.
- I feel itchy under my wool hat.

SEEING: Notice the varying pitch of rooflines, the quality of light, the play of shadows, and the movement of small animals. List the things you see. Be specific.

Example:
- I see the woodpecker hole in the old maple tree.
- I see the gray squirrel running along the old stonewall.
- I see the red paint peeling off the side of the barn.
- I see the school bus passing with children peering out the dirty rear window.
- I see distinct shadows of the bare trees on snow.

LISTENING: Hear the sounds around you. Find them all equally important. State in your head all the sounds that you hear beginning with your footsteps.

Example:
- I hear my feet hitting the road.
- I hear dry reeds rustling in the marsh.
- I hear a metal plow scraping icy ground.
- I hear the low roar of an engine as a plane passes overhead.
- I hear a dog barking at the top of a long driveway.

SMELLING: Practice inhaling deeply through the nose. Have an olfactory banquet. Smell all the scents around you and list them in your head. Be specific.

Example:

- I smell the pungent odor of cow manure.
- I smell wet, cut grass.
- I smell diesel exhaust from a salt truck.
- I smell the spring thaw.
- I smell body odor.

TASTING: Inhale through your mouth, keeping your tongue pressed down. What do you taste?

Example:

- I taste the air, subtle but strong.
- I taste peppermint gum.
- I taste something metallic.
- I taste the residue of my lunch.

Take time to use all your senses to open more fully into the road. How does this change the focus of your attention and expand your experience of walking?

Weaving the Tapestry of Vermont

Roads are often a line connecting where we are to where we are going. If we are in a rush, the "best" road is the one that provides the straightest and most efficient route. The highway does a fantastic job of cutting through the landscape to find the most direct way to progress. Its smooth, paved line blasts through hillside and pushes aside any barrier that slows down its forward-moving momentum.

The back roads of Vermont rebel against straight lines as they follow the lay of the land. They climb hills, meander along rivers and brooks, skirt along open cornfields, hide under the canopy of dark woods, shrink into lanes, and sometimes dwindle into secret foot trails. The back roads connect farms to forests, mountains to valleys. They are blind to class. Rich and poor live side by side separated by a stonewall crumbling under time. Their treasures demonstrate how present blends past and future: yesterday's forgotten cellar holes border tomorrow's foundations. When we walk the roads, we enter the tapestry by following the thread that binds it all together. My invitation to you: journey along the line that connects opposites by moving in the unified direction of the loop.

How to Follow the Loop:
The Space Between

Journeys are unpredictable, and not always about getting to a destination. They can be as much about process as they are about progress. Focus on the experience of transitioning from beginning to end. A back road walk is an exploration of the space between *being here* and *getting there*.

The "space between" is not an external or objective place. You, the walker, will have your own experience of the space within the journey. Fill the loops with insights, encounters, and secret spots you discover when you allow yourself to open into the road.

The companion text included with each walk is just my experience and serves only as an example or invitation. Each chapter is different because each walk has its own unique feeling. I was different each time I walked. What I noticed and wrote will vary from what you see, think, and feel.

I hope that some of what I discovered wandering and wondering will inspire you to go into *your* space between. Tuck a little journal into your coat pocket. Go deep. Document your soul's journey around Central Vermont's hidden loops.

Transition and the Space Between

When you look at the photographs in this book you might notice that I tend to walk roads during transitional seasons. At those times when the earth lies slumbering, there is a palpable anticipation of the coming of winter or the beginning of spring. My walking seasons, November and March, are known locally as "stick season" and "cabin fever season". They are introverted times of the year. Outdoor enthusiasts are between sports, garden implements are stowed in sheds, leaves have fallen, and the landscape is transparent. Trees lining the road no longer block the field beyond, the distant ridgeline, or the circling hawk. Also conveniently absent from the road are the deep snow, dust, or mud that may impede walkers during the more popular calendar months.

Times of transition are great for wandering and wondering. Seasons of expectancy and yearning, they are periods when being and doing are more balanced. These in-between phases are times when the attraction of hiking, skiing, kayaking, or biking does not compete as fiercely with the simple act of walking.

The unobscured landscape encourages us to become more transparent. There is space to pause, circle ourselves, and explore what lies along the perimeter.

Reasons to walk during the seasons of transition:

- See-through landscape
- Dark silhouettes of wild turkeys gliding across barren fields
- Quiet of nature's slumber
- Smell of wood smoke
- Warm lamp light filtered through drawn curtains
- Crisp, fresh air
- Stark beauty of a tree's skeleton
- No road dust
- Silence

- Geese in formation honking a farewell to summer, or greeting spring
- Anticipation and hope
- Deep thought
- Angular shadows lengthening across rounded meadows of tired snow
- An instant cure for cabin fever
- Momentum in a time of waiting
- Deer bedding down where forest meets field
- Dense clusters of reddish drupes called sumac bobs
- Wind that shifts, causing the eerie creak of scraping branches or the whirling rush of miniature snow tornadoes

Dusty Silence: Looping through Transition

I moved away from Burlington to stay with a friend in the little town of Starksboro. It was my first "stick season" in Vermont, and he was living in a drafty, mouse-infested two-bedroom house on a working dairy farm. Our dining room window overlooked the Hogback Range, which separates Route 116 from Silver Street as you head toward Bristol. The rent was cheap, there was room for a garden, and our dog had a delightful time chasing cows.

Sunday mornings I would step into my snowsuit, fill my pockets with carrots for the neighbors' horses, and wind my way up to a little stone Quaker meetinghouse perched among the Starksboro hills. Folk singing, silent worship, and the heat of the woodstove would warm my body and soul. It was a quiet, transitional time for me and for the surrounding, sheltering terrain.

I spent much of that time walking. Roads that appeared to end would, upon closer investigation, dwindle to snowmobile trails or old logging routes, always allowing passage farther and deeper into both the outer surroundings and my internal circumstance. Faith and movement would inevitably guide me to the top of another road leading back down to my starting point. Removed from the flow of time, hidden in dusty silence, Vermont revealed its true nature on those twisting roads. Treasures emerged: old cellar holes next to overgrown lilac trees, timid black bears lumbering along the backs of fallow fields, orchards heavy with ripe fruit, family graveyards tucked into odd corners, abandoned houses filled with photographs of strangers …

I walked, calling out my existential questions to the road. Who am I? Where am I going? What should I do? Questions without answers, asked on looping roads without ends. The questioning, like the walking, had virtue beyond answers and arrivals. Walking on roads taught me that evolving and growing are more about reclaiming and remembering than learning anything new. Finding the hidden treasures along those dusty roads, I uncovered the beautiful, forgotten parts of myself. Loop walks guided me, after many years of running away, back to the place where I started. In this continual act of returning, I led myself home.

The Road Namesake

It's nice when a name makes sense. Visit suburbs across America, and you'll see street names that have nothing to do with what's actually there. "Elm Street" has no elms; a stroll down "Glendale Road" reveals neither glen, nor dale. This pervasive lack of authenticity is what that gives many suburbs a depressingly artificial feeling.

In rural Vermont the names of roads reliably represent what is there now, provide a succinct history of what was there in the past, or serve as simple directions. The road that connects Marshfield to Calais is called the Calais Road if you're heading toward Calais or the Marshfield Road if you're heading toward Marshfield.

Many back road names in this book end with the word *hill*. Notice how your hamstrings feel after you're done walking and you'll understand why. *Brook Roads* usually follow the curves of rushing mountain streams. There are many *Common Roads*, because village centers often include a common area where you will find the schoolhouse, cemetery, and what used to be communal, shared land. *Common Roads* are generally the oldest routes, since they were the main thoroughfares for early settlers to get from outlying areas to a burgeoning village center. A *Main Street* will most likely take you through the middle part of town, as in the walk through Warren Village.

If a road's name includes a landmark such as Robinson Cemetery, Old West Church, or Bliss Pond, you will quite likely pass that road's eponym during your journey. Roads that don't reference an obvious landmark or topological feature may be even more deeply rooted in regional history. In the case of Laird Pond Road, outside of Plainfield, the erstwhile pond has returned to marshland after storms washed away the dam on Nasmith Brook. If you want to dive even deeper into the story of a road, visit the local cemetery. The names of the founding families, memorialized on the lichen-covered headstones, are also the names of the roads along which these households spent generation after generation living, working, loving, and dying. Pause from your walk and listen: you can almost hear the soft sighing of their stoic striving.

Saved by the Loop: Wondering into the Past

Recess was always the hardest part of the school day. Fearful that I would be left out of the Chinese jump rope game, I would drift around the playground alone. Middle school exacerbated those fears. My locker neighbor would never let me put my jacket and lunch box away while she was in the same hallway.

Anytime there was unstructured time to socialize, I became anxious and didn't know what to say. Because my peers could spot my self-doubt, I became an easy target. It got to a point where I would hide in the bathroom, climb a tree, or take a nap in the nurse's office during recess so I wouldn't have to go through the adolescent anxiety of trying to fit in and find my place among my classmates.

Helping kids to develop "healthy lifestyle choices" was a big trend back in the late eighties. No more soda pop in the vending machines and a new program to encourage walking. At the beginning of sixth grade, we each received a large index card with numbers that were punched every time we completed a lap around the quarter-mile track. When a student finished a certain number of miles, her name was entered into a lottery. During monthly assembly programs names were chosen from an enormous hat and the winner got to come up on stage and pick a prize.

Since I can't remember any of the prizes, they were obviously not very remarkable. And heading down the long auditorium aisles in front of the whole student body felt like a nightmare, especially when other children knew it was because of an obsessive walking hobby. But still, the walking was always worth it.

I would head out to the track after devouring my lunch. I started looking forward to recess because I could escape into the rhythm of walking. During that quarter mile the school day, my teasing peers, and my social studies research paper would disappear. I could simply continue to complete laps around the track and watch the holes multiply on my card.

That gravel track was my refuge. It allowed me to be in my own thoughts and notice the small things I might have overlooked: Like the autumn winds or my oddball science teacher's vegetable garden…

Walking was healthy, and not just for my body. Time away from *doing* gave me the freedom to enjoy *being in the moment* as I moved through space. It gave me an opportunity to allow my thoughts to wander, to breathe deeply, and to remember who I was. The "healthy lifestyle choices" program became yet another '80s fad, but walking is still the activity to which I return when I need perspective, mental balance, and access to a sense of emotional safety.

PART 2:

Wanderings

Section 1: Mad River Valley

 **Moretown**

How To Get There:

From Interstate 89, take Exit 9. Merge onto Center Road and turn left onto US-2 East. Enter into Middlesex and turn right onto Vermont 100B South. Follow 100B to Moretown Village and take a sharp left before the Mobil station onto Moretown Mountain Road. Reach junction with Moretown Common Road.

If you want a short but gorgeous stroll, stick with the smaller loop. This walk starts at Moretown Common and is filled with treasures such as the Moretown Common Cemetery, a converted schoolhouse, and views across the Mad River Valley. The middle part of Farnham Road, marked by a hidden waterfall off to the right, is very steep and not maintained. In the winter this means walking through deep snow. While this strenuous part of the walk is short, and can usually be done without snowshoes, it is best to choose this walk when there is not heavy snow cover.

If you enjoy a walk that begins with a nice climb, park at the junction of Moretown Common Road and Mountain Road and explore the larger loop. The descent down Hathaway from Moretown Common is delightful, with big maples lining much of the road, a beautiful ridgeline off to the left, and some timeworn homesteads tucked behind old stone walls. Be careful when you turn right to head down the last section on Moretown Mountain Road. Though unpaved, this curvy mountain road traverses the gap that cuts through the ridge into Northfield Falls, and is well traveled by cars. People drive fast down the mountain, and the sharp bends can conceal walkers. While proper walking etiquette is to walk toward traffic, do not hesitate to cross over to the other side on the blind curves.

Moretown Loop

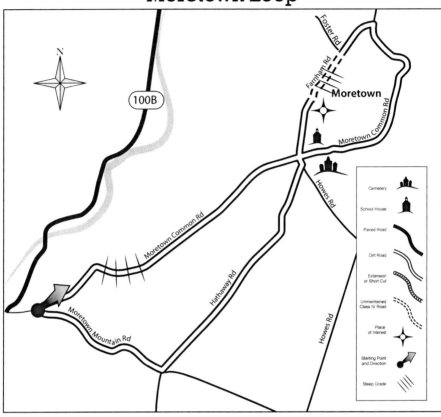

Moretown Common–Combined Loop 5.5 miles

Moretown Mountain Loop-3.6 miles

- Park at the bottom of Moretown Common Road
- Head up Moretown Common Road for approximately 1.5 miles until you reach Moretown Common.
- Turn right onto Howes Road
- Take the first right onto Hathaway Road
- Turn right onto Moretown Mountain Road
- Follow Moretown Mountain Road to junction with Moretown Common Road

Moretown Common Loop-1.9 miles

- Park across from converted schoolhouse near junction of Farnham Road and Moretown Common Road
- Walk up (north) Farnham Road
- Continue onto unmaintained, steep section and pass junction with Foster road
- Turn right onto Moretown Common Road
- Arrive back at schoolhouse after passing the Moretown Common Cemetery

A Moment on the Road

It was early March, right before sugaring season when the crispness of winter mixes with the moist expectation of approaching thaw. I decided to extend the usual Moretown loop by continuing down Howes Road to end farther up Moretown Mountain Road. At the edge of the common area just past Hathaway Road is an old farm with a ramp leading up to the entrance of the hayloft.

It was midday, and the sun was high and bright, casting shadows across the late winter snow. As I approached the barn I could see something suspended from the large roof beams. The road was quiet, and the spinning of the shadow cast directly under the entrance was like a clock pendulum marking cadence. Hanging from one leg, with a tiny trickle of fresh blood beginning to congeal on the corner of its mouth, was a healthy, thick-coated coyote.

I heard a tractor coming down from the fields behind the farmhouse and waited for the farmer to approach. He seemed wary of my presence, but my curiosity regarding the coyote quelled any of his worries about a trespassing stranger. He told me the coyote had been feasting on his livestock for weeks. After killing the predator with a good shot, he said the hanging would be fair warning for his furry buddies to stay off the property. I wished him well as I walked past his pasture full of pigs, cows, and chickens. They could now rest easy knowing that they were, at least temporarily, out of harm's way. Farmer, domestic prey, cunning predator: the classic story and the cycle of life all glimpsed within a moment on the road.

Waitsfield Common Loop

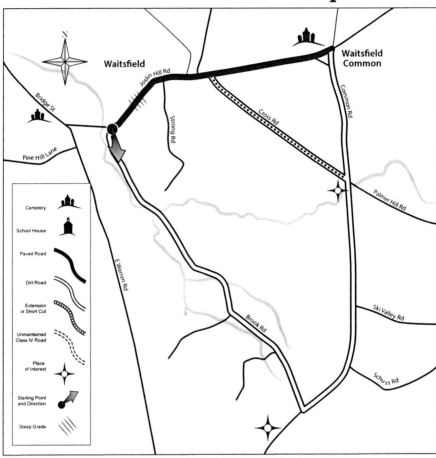

Waitsfield Common Loop - 4 miles
- Park near junction of Joslin Hill Road and Brook Road
- Turn right onto Brook Road
- Turn left onto Common Road
- Turn left onto Joslin Hill Road
- Reach junction with Brook Road

Shorter Loop (missing Waitsfield Common using Cross Road as shortcut)
3.6 miles
- Turn right onto Brook Road
- Turn left onto Common Road
- Turn left onto Cross Road
- Turn left onto Joslin Hill Road

Walk #2 Waitsfield

How to get there:

From the south: Take Exit 9 off of Interstate 89. Turn left onto Center Road. Turn left onto Route 2 East. Go through Middlesex and turn right onto Vermont 100B South. Pass through Moretown and continue onto VT 100 South/ Main Street. Enter into Waitsfield and turn left onto Bridge Street. Go over the covered bridge and turn a slight left onto Joslin Hill Road.

From the north: From I-89, Take Exit 10 and merge onto Route VT 100 South. Turn left onto North Main Street (Route 2 East/Route 100 South). Continue through Waterbury Village. After the bridge, turn right to continue following Route 100 South. At the junction with Route 100B, turn right to stay on Route 100. Enter into Waitsfield and turn left onto Bridge Street. Slight left onto Joslin Hill Road.

This loop is a charming and moderate walk with continuous views across the Mad River Valley. Flanked by the Northfield Ridge and the mountains holding Sugarbush and Mad River Glen ski resorts, this walk ascends up to a ridge road, passes through historic Waitsfield Common, and then ends with a mile-long paved descent on Joslin Hill.

When you pass through the village of Waitsfield and cross over the covered bridge heading toward East Warren, you quickly enter into the back roads of the majestic Mad River Valley. Joslin Hill is the first left off the East Warren Road, and the loop begins at Brook Road immediately on your right.

Brook Road is a wooded and somewhat steep dirt road that follows the drainage up to the top of the small ridge. While the loop heads left on Common Road, it will be worth your time to detour right about a quarter of a mile or less to climb up to the top of the rise. At the top of the hill sits two homesteads lined with old maple trees and dry stack stone walls. While both still are working farms, one whispers of a time past while the other embraces the Vermont of the future. The entire Common Road, all the way into historical Waitsfield Common, offers amazing views of the Green Mountains and Mad River Valley.

Follow the Common Road to the junction with Cross Road, and notice Skinner Barn on the corner. With its classic post and beam structure, this barn was built in 1791 and still functions as a cultural hub, hosting a variety of theatre, dance, and music performances during the summer. To learn more, check out the website at http://www.theskinnerbarn.com/

You can shorten the loop by skipping Waitsfield Common and taking Cross Road down to Joslin Hill. If you would like to walk the entire four miles, continue straight through this junction and climb past the gorgeous old farm and its surrounding pastureland. Descend into Waitsfield Common through a canopy of old maples and pass the Von Trapp Greenhouses.

Make a left onto Joslin Hill and take a few moments to explore this historic corner. Stroll through the old cemetery or have a snack on the site of the original 1794 Waitsfield Settlement.

Leave the common and descend down the mile-long paved section of Joslin Hill. Look out for the funky metal sculptures about three-quarters of the way down on the left.

Walk #3   Fayston—The Valley under Burnt Rock

How to get there:

From Waterbury or Exit 10 off of I-89: Follow Route 100 South to the intersection with Route 100 B. Turn right and continue on Route 100 South for about one mile. Turn right onto North Fayston Road. Follow North Fayston Road for about three miles to reach North Fayston Cemetery. Randell Road will be on the left.

From Montpelier or Exit 9 off of I-89: Take Route 2 into Middlesex to Route 100 B. Turn left and follow Route 100 B South through Moretown Village. When 100 B becomes Route 100 South, continue straight for about one mile. Turn right onto North Fayston Road. Follow North Fayston Road for about three miles to reach North Fayston Cemetery. Randell Road will be on the left.

●

This is an 'introverted loop'* that weaves through the hillside of the Mad River Valley coming out of the woods and into a magical, pastoral valley. Fayston is a quiet town covering about 36.5 square miles tucked between scenic Route 100 and Route 17. The walk takes you through the history of Fayston as you stroll past two old schoolhouses and begin at the village cemetery.

Begin near North Fayston cemetery across from the converted schoolhouse. Turn left on Randell Road and descend into a moist nook. The road crosses over a bridge and then continues to curve and wind steeply into the wooded hills of the Mad River Valley. The mixed woods are dark with stands of coniferous trees. During the curvy ascent, there are only a couple of ridgeline views. Turn around and walk backwards if you need encouragement that you are making progress and want to catch a good view.

During the "introverted" part of the walk, where it seems that you are walking through the leeward side of the hill, Randall Road will run into Center Fayston Road. Take a right and eventually meander down to the junction with Murphy Road. Stay on Center Fayston and curve to the right as you descend steeply to a bridge over Shepard Brook.

At this point the road opens to reveal a protected valley in the middle

Fayston Loop

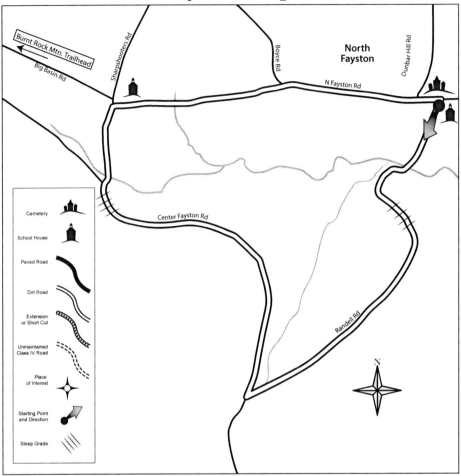

Fayston Loop - 4.1 miles

- Park near the North Fayston Cemetery
- Turn onto Randell Road
- Turn right onto Center Fayston Road
- At converted schoolhouse, follow the main road right and continue on North Fayston Road
- Reach junction with Randell Road

of the hills. Walk through the valley to the corner of Center Fayston Road and Big Basin Road. Big Basin is a smaller dirt road that leads to the Burnt Rock Trailhead. For an entirely different adventure, this 5.2-mile round trip hike leads up to a lesser-known vista lending to some of the best views on the Long Trail.

At the junction with Big Basin is a green and white converted schoolhouse. Once, when I was walking the loop in late winter, the landscape was cloaked in a silent, snow-covered slumber. Approaching the schoolhouse from across the valley, I could hear reggae music and spotted many wooden, painted stars scattered throughout the property.

A dark-haired woman and her child were out in the field on a wooden toboggan and approached me as I reached this unusual junction. She told me that the schoolhouse had been in her family since 1943, and about ten years ago she moved in full time. We discussed the history of her little corner and how the natives used to cut through the verdant valley on their way to Burnt Rock. She told me that the schoolhouse, located at the edge of the valley, was indeed the center of a special loop.

It was an energetic gathering place and a sacred crossroad. If you need to rest or want a snack, this surely is the place to linger.

After staying right at the junction, continue on Center Fayston Road. Leave the valley, pass by the town garage, and tuck back into the hills. The rest of the walk toward Randell Road is more open, with views to the right. Pass by the picturesque Vermont Icelandic Horse Farm before finding your way back to the cemetery.

* What I mean by an introverted loop

When dark woods shade a road and the climbing is steep, my focus draws inward. Once, on this walk I was feeling especially vulnerable and self-reflective. I worked through some inner doubt and was in a mental space where I needed to feel separate and protected.

It was interesting how this was reflected in what I noticed. This loop felt nestled in and filled with the stark beauty of bark and stone. My focus was drawn to borders, the outline of shapes, and the texture of objects distinct and jagged. Noticing where I placed my attention, I gained better understanding of my inner journey. By finding inspiration in the bare landscape, I could look into my exposed self and see the loveliness of its rough yet delicate edges.

Trudy Folsom, who lived in Waitsfield, wrote this story for her family in December 1982. James Peck Boyce (1820–1912) was her husband Ike Folsom's great-grandfather. The author's children graciously consented to its use.

How Burnt Rock Mountain Got Its Name

"Ma, have you seen little Blackface? He's not by the gate." Young James Peck Boyce and his brother Caleb burst into the small frame house where their mother sat busy at her flaxwheel, one foot on the cradle where two-month-old Mason lay sleeping. The two boys and their younger sister, Catherine, had just returned from the little district school, a half mile up the road where a total of twenty-six pupils were now enrolled.

"Little Blackface," one of twin lambs born a month earlier, had been disowned by his mother. "If you can raise him, he's yours," David told his oldest son, who joyfully accepted the task. James spent every spare minute with his lamb. As the wobbly little legs grew sturdy, Blackface followed his young master everywhere, except to school. He waited at the split-rail gate when the children ran noisily down the road. But today he was neither at the gate nor with the rest of the flock grazing on the fresh spring grass.

"I'm afraid it's a bear, son," said David Boyce, who returned from his task of pulling tree stumps from a fertile strip of land by Beaver Meadow. "This time of year those old mother bears are pretty hungry after sleeping all winter, and a month-old lamb is mighty tempting."

And so it proved to be. Father and son had gone only a quarter of a mile up the mountain when they came to a bloodstained lamb skin. The bear herself had long since disappeared, probably back to one of the small caves dotting the Fayston mountainside.

"I'll get her!" vowed the boy, fighting to keep back his tears—a twelve-year-old Boyce must not cry. "I'll get every darn bear on this mountain."

And so was born the legend of James Peck Boyce, mighty bear hunter. At first he could only accompany his father or one of his uncles on hunting trips, but by the time he was sixteen—as strong and muscular as any man—hunting bears became an obsession. He spent every spare moment in the Fayston wilderness. When James pulled stumps for his aging uncle Paul, he was rewarded with a muzzle loader for his very own.

One early spring afternoon James and his cousin Dan drove an old bear into a deep cave at the foot of a small peak, one of many along the Fayston Ridge. "Let's smoke him out," said James. After several attempts with a small flintstone, the dry leaves caught, and a good smudge was going. The bear came out all right and was promptly dispatched with a well-aimed shot from the muzzle loader. But the boys had not reckoned with the dryness of the woods that spring. The fire took off, and soon the whole top of the mountain was aflame with a blaze that could be seen for miles. Farmers left their plows and fence building to fight the fire, which was finally extinguished, but not before it had consumed all growth on top of the craggy rocks. Young James and his precious muzzle loader were grounded for the entire summer.

The fire burned so deeply into the thin soil that vegetation never did return. To this day the peak is known as Burnt Rock Mountain.

After his marriage to Mary Boyce, a distant cousin, his expeditions became less frequent, but whenever a farmer lost a new-born lamb, or bear tracks were seen in the neighborhood, James was off on his relentless search. He came to know each small cave where a bear might "hole up." By now he had become known as the mightiest bear hunter in Fayston. Fewer lambs and young calves disappeared in the spring, and mothers felt safer letting their children venture into the woods.

Can we doubt that during his term in Montpelier as representative from Fayston, when he met his fellow lawmakers in the corridors of the State House, more conversation turned to his prowess as a bear hunter than to the enactment of new laws?

When he was ninety years old, two years before his death, James Peck Boyce shot his last bear. Little Blackface was avenged.

Walk #4　Warren

How to get there:

From the north: Take Interstate 89 to Exit 10. Follow Route 100 S/
Route 2 East through Waterbury Village. Turn right after bridge to continue on Route 100 South. Turn right at junction with Route 100B to
continue following Route 100 South through Waitsfield. Turn left into
Warren Village. Park at the Park and Ride on historic Main Street.

From the south: Take Interstate 89 to Middlesex Exit 9 and follow
Route 100B through Moretown. Continue straight onto Route 100
South through Waitsfield and past junction with Route 17. Turn left into
Warren Village. Park at the Park and Ride on historic Main Street.

This loop is a vigorous climb from Warren Village up to East Warren
Four Corners and back down Turner Hill for an unforgettable tour of a
gorgeous section of the Mad River Valley.

Free expression runs rampant in Warren and East Warren Village. The
open, high valley with its expansive views flanked by the Green and
Northfield Mountain Ranges must breed a type of rugged individualism.
The village is filled with old houses brought back to life by funky paint
jobs and artistic renovations. The Warren Store is a unique and eclectic
place complete with a full deli, gallery, clothing store, and bakery. It is a
fantastic way to begin or end this walk. You can check out the updated
menu and other important information on the store's website at: http://
www.warrenstore.com/

Warren is also famous for its liberal politics, epitomized by the annual
Fourth of July parade. The Parade Gallery, located at 270 Main Street, is
a great way to get a glimpse into the personality of the village and to add
another dimension of experience to your walking loop. While the village
of Warren can entice you with its galleries, store, covered bridge, and
swimming holes, this book is about back roads, not village centers. So
without delay, let's begin the journey.

The best place to park is at the Park and Ride lot located at the base of
the village on Main Street. Begin the walk by taking a right onto Brook
Road and heading up through the village. At the edge of the village, as

Warren Loop

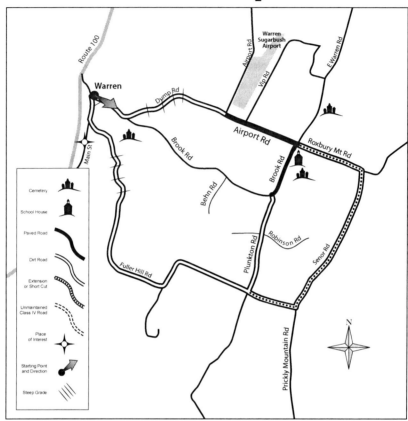

Warren Loop - 6.4 miles, with Senor Road Extensions - 7.5 miles

- Park at the Park and Ride on Main Street
- Head toward village center on Main Street
- Take the first left onto Brook Road
- Turn left onto Dump Road (this is an unmarked dirt road)
- Continue straight onto paved section of Airport Road
- Turn right onto Brook Road at East Warren Four Corners
- Veer left onto Plunkton Road
- Turn right onto Fuller Hill Road
- Slight right onto Main Street (if you want to see the covered bridge, make a left and walk a few hundred feet up Main Street

Senor Extension

- Start from East Warren Store at the Four Corners
- Head straight up Roxbury Mountain Road
- Turn right onto Senor Road
- Turn right onto Fuller Hill Road
- Arrive at junction of Fuller Hill Road and Plunkton Road

Brook Road begins to climb, there is a very steep unmarked dirt road on your left. Turn here and ascend steeply up Dump Road toward East Warren. The road will turn into pavement at the corner of Airport Road. While the climb up Dump Road is strenuous, your work will be paid off with the views found in East Warren, also known as the Four Corners.

After your long climb you might want a break to take in the views and get a snack at the East Warren Community Market located in the old schoolhouse. More information about their food co-op is available at http://www.eastwarrenmarket.com/ The tiny East Warren Cemetery, which borders the store, is definitely worth exploring, with its iron gate and historic gravestones.

To extend the loop, you can ascend up Roxbury Mountain Road and make a right onto Senor Road. This dirt road runs parallel to the well-traveled route through the valley and intersects farther up Fuller Hill, leading you down to the junction with Plunkton Road.

To walk through the middle of the valley, turn right at East Warren Four Corners on Brook Road and make sure to stay left at the fork to continue on Plunkton Road past Blueberry Lake Cross Country Ski Center. Make a right on Fuller Hill Road. After some initial climbing, the road will open into an amazing vista offering 360-degree views of the Mad River Valley and surrounding ranges. Continue through this secret valley and descend through a steep, wooded section back into the village of Warren.

While the loop takes you right on Main Street through the center of town, a quick detour to the left will take you to the Warren covered bridge. I highly recommend this side trip, as the loop would not be complete without a stroll across the bridge and a glance down the river through its rectangular cutaway sides.

A Moment on the Road

As I was catching my breath at the top of Dump Road and taking in the view of the mountain valley, a sprightly group of older women and their dogs came walking up the road, out for a morning stroll. I ended up matching stride and chatting with one of the women as we approached the Four Corners.

She said she had lived in the valley her entire life, and was an Elliot, one of the original families that settled in Warren. She pointed out a favorite apple tree. In her youth she had rested in the shade of its branches on her walk home from school. She showed me the place where she used to cross the cows as she brought them to the milking barn.

She mentioned that her family had owned most of the land around the Four Corners but began selling pieces of it to neighbors to supplement their agricultural livelihood. When I mentioned the word "subdividing," she laughed and said that term was not part of the rural vocabulary back in the valley of her youth. Before "flatlanders" began moving into the valley to build second homes, land was bought from neighbors with a handshake. Money was paid back on the trust system, and no one needed to take loans from the bank or go through a legal process.

In East Warren, progress blends well with tradition. The Elliot family still lives in the valley of their ancestors, and the farm at the Four Corners continues to smell strongly of cow manure and fresh hay, but the schoolhouse has been converted into a local food co-op and home-schooling center.

Section 2: The Backsides of Montpelier

 Walk #5 ## East Montpelier Center

How to get there:

From Montpelier: Continue up Main Street and stay straight through the roundabout. Pass by Towne Hill Road on your right and then Vermont Compost Company on your left. Turn slight right onto Center Road. Park near Doty Cemetery located at the intersection of Dodge Road and Center Road.

This is one of the most historical loop walks covered in the book. It takes you past multiple homesteads and beautiful post-and-beam barns built in the 1800s by the early settlers of East Montpelier. The Ormsbee and Templeton barns are fine examples of gravity barns. The three levels of these vast structures make the best use of gravity by keeping the hay at the top, the cows at ground level, and the manure in the basement. To make the haymow (hayloft) more accessible, these barns have ramps leading to the loft which make it easier to unload large amounts of hay right from the wagon.

Parts of this walk, such as the section of Center Road as you approach its junction with Lyle Young Road, have remained unchanged since the time the area was originally settled. The ancient maples, crumbling stone walls, sprawling farms, and fertile fields give tribute to the labor and love of over two hundred years of rural life in East Montpelier's pastoral valley.

Begin the walk at Doty Cemetery, which for years had been abandoned with many of the old stones removed. Now maintained by Elliot Morse, a gregarious local who is part of one of the most well known families in East Montpelier, Doty is one of only two active cemeteries in the area. Head North on Center Road, quickly approaching Ormsbee Farm, established by the early settlers of the valley and highlighted on the cover of the Spring 2011 edition of *Vermont Life Magazine*. The road

East Montpelier Center Loop

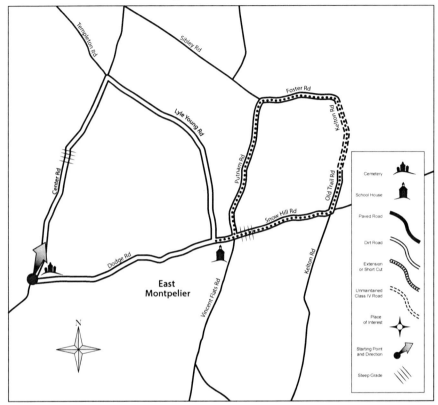

East Montpelier Center—Combined Loop 7.8 miles

Center Loop—4.3 miles

- Park across from Doty Cemetery and head north on Center Road
- Turn right onto Lyle Young Road
- Turn right onto Dodge Road
- Reach junction with Center Road

Four Corners Extension (can be walked as separate loop or attached to the Adamant Village loop)—**3.3 miles**

- Turn left onto Dodge Road from Lyle Young Road
- Turn left at the Four Corners Schoolhouse onto Putnam Road
- Turn right onto Foster Road as Putnam Road turns into Sibley Road
- Foster Road will end at farmhouse with pink and purple doors
- Veer right on trail marked by cement blocks (labeled as Kelton Road on map)
- Continue straight onto maintained section of road (Old Trail Road)
- Turn right onto Snow Hill Road
- Arrive back at junction with Dodge Road

sweeps through well-established farmland and climbs up and through the wooded hillside. Pass by an old homestead complete with a large wooden barn and whitewashed farmhouse with green shutters. Reach the top of the wooded ridge and descend down past an unchanged section of the road lined with ancient maples. Join Lyle Young Road after passing the entrance to Templeton Farm, established in 1877.

Make a right on Lyle Young Road to stroll along an unusually flat and open section of road. Look left to catch a glimpse of the historic Sibley Barn located on the border of Calais and East Montpelier near the village of Adamant. Climb steeply around a sweeping curve and pass by Fairmount Farm before reaching the junction with Dodge Road.

Even if you are not walking the Four Corners extension, I recommend taking a quick detour left. Walk down to the Four Corners to visit the one-room schoolhouse, still used for historical society meetings, Christmas sing-alongs, and other local events.

To complete the loop without the extra three-mile extension, head back up Dodge Road. Walk through a wooded section, and then climb up to East Montpelier Center through fields bordered by mixed woods.

Four Corners Extension

Note: Kelton Road is not plowed in the winter and might be hard to access during times of deep snow.

If you are interested in exploring an unmaintained section of road (otherwise known as a Class IV road), have the stamina to add some more mileage to your walking shoes, and can't get enough of East Montpelier's sprawling homesteads, head left at the Four Corners schoolhouse onto Putnam Road.

Continue on Putnam, dip down over a small bridge and then climb briefly past a barn filled with young animals used for local 4-H clubs. Turn right onto Foster Road. Walk down this small, dead-end road until you reach a large wooden barn and old farmhouse with pink and purple doors. At the farmhouse veer right on the trail (Kelton Road) beginning at the cement barriers that block the road to vehicles. As you sneak between two crumbling walls marking the boundary line between properties, enjoy the remote feel of this rural alley before reaching the maintained section of the road (Old Trail Road). Descend down to the junction with Snow Hill Road and pass the beautiful dry- stack well on your left. Make a right on Snow Hill Road and climb steeply back up to the Four Corners schoolhouse.

Walk #6 Horn of the Moon (East Montpelier)

How to get there:

From Montpelier: Head up Main Street through town and stay straight through the roundabout. Make a quick left on North Street and continue uphill to the junction with Sparrow Farm Road.

Horn of the Moon is a hilly road that begins by crossing over the Wrightsville Reservoir and weaves through a network of delightful East Montpelier roads. It connects the section of Route 14 heading toward Worcester with the County Road in East Montpelier. I asked the head of the East Montpelier historical society where Horn of the Moon got its name. This was his response:

As the story goes, when the first white settlers came to what was then the Town of Montpelier around 1789, there was an old Indian living in the northwest corner of the town. He told someone that when his cow wandered away he found it under the shadow of Long Meadow Hill but told the listener that he found it on the Horn of the Moon.

This response seems like complete nonsense. Maybe the shadow of Long Meadow Hill looks like the Horn of the Moon. I tried to find both myself, but the shadow remained elusive, and I have yet to spot the horn of the moon. But persisting with my search gives me an excuse to return to this loop again and again.

This walk begins less than a ten-minute drive from Montpelier at the corner of North Street and Sparrow Farm Road. Ideally, it should be finished at sunset. The views at this road junction look west toward the Worcester range and make for a gorgeous end to the day. There's also nothing better than completing a walk, watching the sun retreat behind the mountains, and heading into Montpelier for a microbrew and a chat with the locals at Three Penny Taproom. Check out their website at http://www.threepennytaproom.com/

The walk itself is perfectly balanced, starting out with a wooded, modest ascent up North Street. Notice the whitewashed farmhouses, gnarled maple trees, and dry stack walls that line the road. Throughout the walk old and new are seamlessly woven. The silence of the old walls grounds

Horn of the Moon Loop

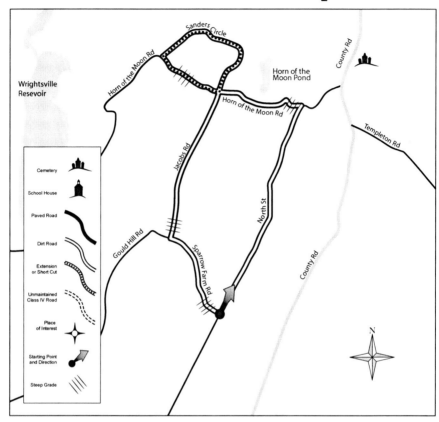

Horn of the Moon Loop (East Montpelier)—4.6 miles
With Sanders Circle Extension—6.4 miles

Horn of the Moon Loop
- Park on North Street near junction with Sparrow Farm Road
- Head straight up North Street
- Turn left onto Horn of the Moon Road
- Head left onto Jacobs Road
- Turn left onto Sparrow Farm Road
- Arrive back at junction with North Street

Sanders Circle Extension—1.8 miles
- Arrive at junction of Horn of the Moon Road, Jacobs Road, and Sanders Circle
- Turn right onto Sanders Circle
- Take left onto Horn of the Moon Road
- Arrive back at junction

the rhythmic sounds of rural life still active even in the "month of wait-ing" (March)… The Casella trash truck grinding through gears to get up the icy roads, the scraping of the plow making better access for the Montpelier commuters, the soft bubbling sound of the road breathing as the ice thaws, and the bark of golden retrievers dutifully announcing a stranger's passing.

Take North Street until it ends and turn left on Horn of the Moon Road. After climbing up a steep, short hill, the road dramatically curves, exposing expansive and sweeping views of the valley and the loom-ing Worcester range. The rest of the walk, including the Sanders Circle Extension (taking you back farther into the bowl of the valley), is a feast for both the eyes and the soul. Complete with open views, fields mixed with woods, and a hilly but not too steep terrain, this loop has it all. The walk ends in a charming fashion as you turn left off Jacobs Road onto Sparrow Farm Road. The final leg climbs back up to North Street, pass-ing by Sparrow Farm and continuing along a row of large sugar maples.

Walk #7 North Montpelier

How to get there:

From Montpelier: Follow Route 2 East. Pass the junction with Route 302 and continue toward East Montpelier. After the Mobil Station, turn onto Route 14 North. Turn left onto Factory Street. Park near the junction with Gray Road.

North Montpelier was not established as a rural community like neighboring East Montpelier. Kingsbury Branch, one of the seven tributaries feeding the Winooski River, was first dammed in 1792 to create a sawmill. This dam has been used ever since as the center of industry, and the Woolen Mill in North Montpelier was the hub of the town's existence until its closing in 1969. Factory Street once held a large boarding house to supply shelter for the mill workers.

North Montpelier Loop

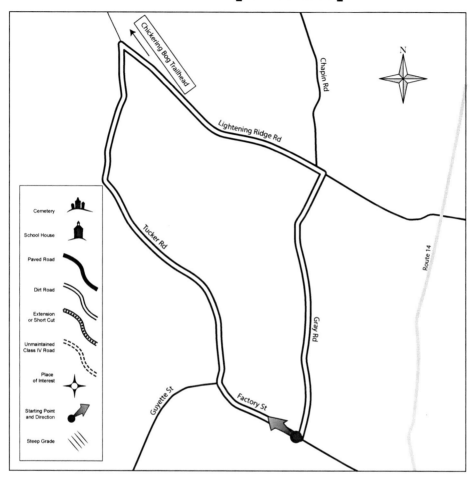

North Montpelier Loop—3.5 miles

- Park on Factory Street near junction with Gray Road
- Walk up Factory Street toward Tucker Road
- Take the first right onto Tucker Road
- Turn right onto Lightening Ridge Road
- Take the first right onto Gray Road
- Reach junction with Factory Street

This easy, accessible walk is only three-tenths of a mile away from the entrance to Chickering Bog, a unique "bobbing bog" maintained by the Nature Conservancy, where the vegetation floats on the top of water. Information and directions to Chickering Bog can be found on the Vermont Nature Conservancy's website.

Park near the junction of Factory Street and Gray Road. Head west on Factory Street along a high fenced property before veering right onto Tucker Road. Climb gently along this small, quiet road through mixed fields and woods until reaching the junction with Lightening Ridge Road.

I had assumed Lightening Ridge got its name from an unusual amount of electrical activity hitting houses high on the hill. The real story is that this steep road was used by horse teams moving granite from quarry to plant. On steep sections of the road, especially during mud season when the road seemed bottomless, the drivers would have to "lighten" the load so the horse teams could successfully pull the granite over the ridge.

Turn right on Lightening Ridge, enjoy expansive views, and pass by Lilley Hill Farm, with its domed-shaped barn. Descend down this large dirt road to the junction with Gray Road, and turn right before reaching the entrance to Calais Elementary School. Walk along Gray Road until you reach the junction with Factory Street to complete the loop.

Section 3: Calais

 Adamant

How to get there:

From Montpelier: Head up Main Street and continue straight through the traffic circle. Stay slight left to continue onto County Road. Turn right onto Haggett Road. Pass Martin Road on your left. Enter into Adamant Village. Adamant Co-op is at the junction with Center Road. Park in Adamant Co-op parking area.

I went into the Adamant Co-op to grab a quick snack for my walk and to see if I could get some information about the history of the village. The co-op is not just a collectively run grocery store but is a left-leaning political hub, local art gallery, post office, and gathering place for people living in and passing through the village. During the fifteen minutes I was at the store, every person that entered, ranging from six to eighty, knew each other by name. While I advocate for walking during the "see through season" (November and March), there is much to do in Adamant, *other than walking*, all year round.

- Blackfly Festival in late May
- Friday night cookouts on the community porch
- Concerts at the Adamant Music School
- A picnic in the sculpture park
- Quarryworks Community Theatre
- Adamant Winter Music Series at the Community Club

With all this culture and community, you would think Adamant was an urban mecca instead of a small, rural village surrounded by dirt roads with a population just over sixteen hundred. You can find out more at **http://www.adamantcoop.org/**

Adamant Loop

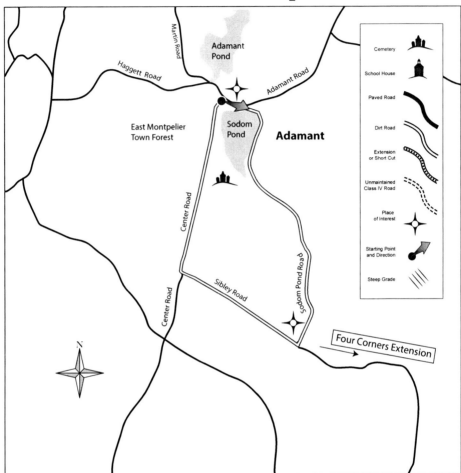

Adamant (Sodom Pond) Loop—4.0 miles

- Park at Adamant Co-op in Adamant Village
- Head east up Adamant Road
- Take first right onto Sodom Pond Road
- Turn right onto Sibley Road
- Turn right onto Center Road
- Reach junction with Adamant Road

* The Four Corners Extension, an additional 3.3 miles, can be attached to this walk as well as the East Montpelier Center Loop. This is done by taking a left at the corner of Sodom Pond Road and Sibley Road and then following directions listed in the East Montpelier section *

Walking the Loop

Head up Adamant Road and quickly veer right on Sodom Pond Road. Skirt along the perimeter of the pond, crossing the border into East Montpelier. Enjoy a flat, quiet stroll up to the junction of Sibley Road, where you will find the historic Sibley Farm, built in 1899. Notice the "viewing" cupola at the top of the barn. A long- time resident of the area told me that it was built with a staircase and seats so that the farmer could "best view his herd, the land, and the productivity of his workers."

As you turn right to head northwest toward Center Road, you will see the other side of the barn with its classic high drive, which allows hay to be driven directly into the loft. Just like many Vermont dairy farms, Sibley Farm is no longer an active dairy but still raises cows or "replacement heifers" to sell to other dairy farms for milking.

Continue down an open, wide stretch of road surrounded by fields and farmland. Curve past a homestead and then up along an active sugar bush (stand of maples tapped for syrup) to reach the junction with Center Road.

Make a right on Center Road and continue to follow the large sugar bush as you head north back to the village. Pass by a small orchard, working farm, and two old farmhouses before reaching the hillier section of this otherwise flat stroll. Descend briefly over a small stream and climb up past Peck Cemetery, tucked back into a field on your right. Complete the loop by descending down past Sodom Pond and back to the co-op and village center.

Some history of Adamant, taken with permission, from the Adamant Cooperative website:

In 1858 a crossroads appeared on an old Washington County map complete with a sawmill and six houses but no name. Granite quarries opened there in 1880, bringing workers from Scotland and Canada. A boarding house built near the quarry along with several other houses warranted a Post Office, which was called Sodom.

On Sunday mornings, a curtain was pulled across the bar in Barney's Hall, the gathering place for dances and plays, so religious services could be held without distraction.

A schoolhouse was built in 1895; until then, classes had been held on the upper floor of a resident's house. By 1896, at least forty men were employed in six different quarries, and, at one time, 50 horses were stabled in the village of Sodom.

Albert Bliss, who refused to receive mail with the unsavory postmark of Sodom, petitioned the Post Office to change its name. Permission was given on the condition that the chosen name be unlike any other post office in the state. In 1905 Sodom was renamed Adamant, chosen for the granite quarries and the hardness of their stone, reportedly "A name perhaps as hard but not as wicked."

During the winter of 1934–1935, a local pastor gathered a group of neighbors to discuss starting a co-operative to buy groceries and create a market for local produce. In August of 1935, after eleven families each contributed five dollars to provide working capital, the Adamant Cooperative was incorporated. The Co-op rented space from Minnie Horr, who operated both the store and the post office out of her house, and purchased the building in 1940 for $600.

Walk #9 Maple Corner

How to get there:

From Montpelier: Head up Main Street and continue straight at the traffic circle. Stay slight left to continue onto County Road and follow approximately ten miles until the paved road turns to dirt. Maple Corner Store will be on your left.

The walks start out at the Maple Corner Store, which has been open continuously since 1900. When the stagecoach road ended, the population center moved from Kent Corner to Maple Corner. Artie and Nancy, who own and run the store, put out a regular newsletter of local happenings, run community wine tastings, and are usually around to greet customers with delicious homemade muffins, hot pizza, or deli sandwiches. An addition was recently placed in the back of the store to house the Whammy Bar, a cozy spot to indulge in local beer and comfort food.

Maple Corner itself is a hub for community events. The red barn on the corner greets visitors with a painting of a cow whose costume constantly changes with the seasons. The blue barn hosts community theatre, Halloween masquerade parties, and a sculptural stone truck created by local artist Chris Miller. Curtis Pond sports immaculately maintained ice hockey rinks, always crowded on winter evenings and weekends. The community center is maintained through a fund created by the sale of the now famous "Men of Maple Corner" wall calendars in which the locals posed in their birthday suits holding strategically placed chain saws and fishing poles.

This part of Calais deserves an entire day! I would suggest giving yourself time to explore the magic of the roads, enjoying Curtis Pond, meeting the friendly and creative locals, and truly experiencing what happens if you linger "where the pavement ends."

A Moment on the Road

Like many old cemeteries, Robinson Cemetery lies above the hub of a village. It overlooks Kent Corner, a historic and beautiful intersection in the heart of Calais. The six Kent brothers and their children were

Maple Corner Loop

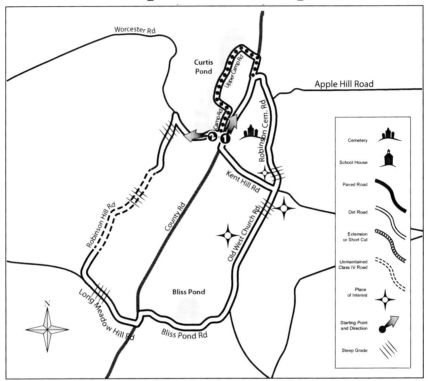

1. Classic Maple Corner Loop—2.5 miles

- Park at Maple Corner Store
- Head northeast through village on West County Road toward Robinson Cemetery Road
- Slight right onto Robinson Cemetery Road
- Pass Old Mill and take right onto Kent Hill Road
- Join back with County Road at the Maple Corner Store

With small extension along Curtis Pond—approximately 3 miles

- Take first left after Maple Corner onto Worcester Road
- Take first right after Blue Barn onto Camp Road
- There is a small section of unmaintained road between Camp and Upper Camp Road *
- Take right onto County Road
- Take first left onto Robinson Cemetery Road
- Turn right onto Kent Hill Road
- Reach junction with County Road at the Maple Corner Store

2. Bliss Pond/Old West Church—6 miles

- Park at Maple Corner Store and continue up County Road
- Take first left onto Worcester Road
- Turn left onto Robinson Hill Road
- The middle section of this road is unmaintained and not plowed in the winter*
- Turn left onto Long Meadow Hill Road
- Turn left onto County Road
- Take immediate right onto Bliss Pond Road
- Turn left onto Old West Church Road
- Turn left onto Kent Hill Road
- Reach junction with County Road at the Maple Corner Store

This loop can be combined with the Maple Corner Loop by going straight through Kent Corner onto Robinson Cemetery Road and then turning left onto County Road to head back to Maple Corner. The entire loop with this extension would be approximately 7.5 miles *

the early settlers of this part of Washington County. They developed a bustling commercial center along the stagecoach road, which led all the way up to Canada. Along with other early Calais settlers such as the Robinson and Bliss families, they built and operated the sawmill, tavern, shoe and boot shop, I & A Kent Store, subsistence farms, and the old churches that still stand amongst the maples centuries later. The distinctively named Remember Kent (1775–1855) is buried in the Robinson Cemetery, along with the other patriarchs of Calais.

I was walking the Maple Corner Loop late one day after work. It was during the witching hour surrounding sunset, where time seems to extend as the shadows lengthen and day transitions into evening. I decided to balance my movement with stillness and stepped off the road to lie in the soft moss amongst the gravestones. I had read about Remember Kent and how he helped to construct the Old West Church and the other historic structures in the area. I had this nostalgic idea that Remember was the quieter of the Kent brothers, hard working and modest. I would often notice his gravestone as I passed by the Kent family plot and ponder what life might have been like hundreds of years ago.

On this particular evening as I walked through the cemetery, I noticed something unique as I passed by his grave. I had an unusual feeling of being pulled away from the present, coupled with the sensation of a quiet energy leaving the cemetery with me as I continued down the road. It seemed, as I passed the old Robinson Farm and down along the millpond and sawmill, that my footsteps were not solitary. I could swear I heard the sound of heavy boots walking next to me, and I felt comforted that maybe the spirit of Remember had decided to briefly escort me on my sunset stroll.

What I find most amazing about Calais, and specifically Maple Corner, is the same sense of community that allowed the early settlers to be successful in creating their rural hamlets still exists among the creative folks who call the corner their home.

Walk #10 Bliss Pond / Old West Church

How to get there:

From Montpelier: Head up Main Street and continue straight at traffic circle. Stay slight left to continue onto County Road and follow approximately ten miles until the paved road turns to dirt. Maple Corner Store will be on your left.

This is a longer loop from the Maple Corner Store, which takes you on a varied and historic meander over Robinson Hill, alongside Bliss Pond, past the famous Old West Church, and down through Kent Corner. Walk through Maple Corner and make a left on the road to Worcester, pass the Big Blue Barn as well as Curtis Pond Beach and boat launch area. Climb briefly up past the pond to Robinson Hill Road and turn left.

Ascend steeply toward the Robinson homestead along open pastureland with epic views to the north and east. Two large dogs might be outside at the top of the hill, but they are behind an invisible fence and will only bark.

As you enter the wooded, remote section of road, notice the waterfall on your right. The road is not maintained after the former farmhand house (now a private residence). You might need snowshoes if you are walking in winter, although snowmobiles and cross-country skiers usually pack the trail down. The trail turns back into a maintained road at a classic white farmhouse close to the junction with Long Meadow Hill.

Make a left on Long Meadow Hill and descend the steep, heavily wooded road. Pass a junction with the VAST trail system before reaching County Road. Turn left, cross over the paved road, and make a quick right onto Bliss Pond Road.

The remaining roads (Bliss Pond, Old West Church, and Kent Hill) form the border around Calais Town Forest, a locally maintained labyrinth of trails taking you along the backside of Bliss Pond and through a delightful bog. Old West Church Road is a beautiful and historic road that runs past a brick farmhouse, an archetypal gravity barn, rolling pastureland lined with sugar maples, and Old West Church itself. The

church is always open to the public and a quick trip through the interior is highly recommended. To read about this historical monument visit the National Park Service website at **http://www.nps.gov/nr/travel/centralvermont/cv40.htm**

Stroll down into Kent Corner to reach the historic Kent Tavern and Ira Kent House. To extend your adventure and connect the loop with the Classic Maple Corner walk, stay straight onto Robinson Cemetery Road and turn left onto County Road. To head directly back to the store, make a left onto Kent Hill Road and finish your journey with an easy half-mile section along Kent Flats.

How to get there:

From Montpelier: Take the County Road approximately ten miles into Maple Corner. Turn right onto Kent Hill Road. Follow 1.25 miles to Gospel Hollow. The Calais Town Hall will be on your right at the bottom of the long hill.

Gospel Hollow, also known as Pekin, is the geographic center of Calais and home of the Calais Town Hall and Town Clerk's Office. The Town Hall, housed in the Christian Church Building, was built in 1866. Town meetings have been held in this historic structure since 1868. The reverend's house is still standing and currently occupied as a private residence located on the corner of Kent Hill and Elmslie Road.

The residents of Calais vote amongst the Town Hall's sturdy, wooden pews. I happened to be living in Calais when President Obama took of-

Gospel Hollow Loop

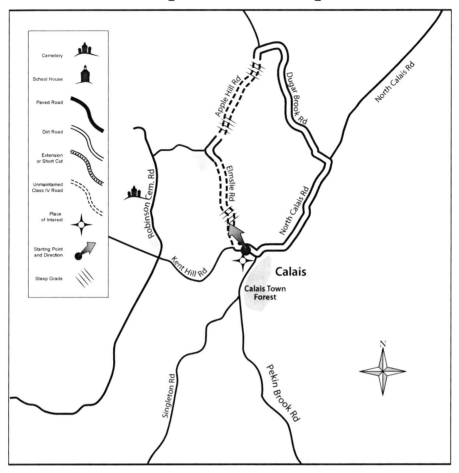

Gospel Hollow Loop—4.5 Miles

- Park at the Calais Town Hall
- Head up Kent Hill Road and take first right onto Elmslie Road
- Head north on Elmslie Road (Majority of this road is unmaintained and steep)
- Turn right onto Apple Hill Road (Parts of this road are unmaintained)
- Turn right onto Dugar Brook Road
- Turn right onto North Calais Road
- Turn right onto Kent Hill Road.

fice in 2008. While people in the big cities waited in long lines to vote, I strolled down Kent Hill to the old church nestled in Gospel Hollow. Volunteers greeted voters with cookies and fresh apple pie. We enjoyed homemade sweets while crouching over the wooden seats penciling in the paper ballets. Leaving the whitewashed Church to ascend out of its shady hollow, I could see my hope for change reflected in the slanted, evening light rising up the hillside.

Walking the Loop

This is a wooded, remote walk through the lower hollow of Calais along its meandering waterways and surrounding marshland. The first half of the walk down Elmslie and Apple Hill is vigorous with steep, unmaintained sections. The last half, along Dugar and Pekin Brook Roads, is flat and tucks you between hillside and the edge of secluded marshland.

This loop is very different from the open, historic walks starting from Maple Corner. It follows old stone walls, the constant sound of rushing water, and verdant wetlands filled with birdsong and dancing reeds. Make sure you bring an extra layer, as this loop is mostly in the shade and can be a bit chilly. Since part of the walk is on steep, unmaintained roads, this loop is not recommended for midwinter walking.

Walk #12　North Calais

How to get there:

From Montpelier: Follow Route 2 East/ Berlin Street to Route 14. Turn left on Route 14 and follow for approximately eight miles into East Calais. Make left onto Moscow Woods Road. Turn right on North Calais Road. Take a sharp left at Nelson Pond Road. Take the first right onto GAR Road and park at the Mirror Lake Access.

North Calais has a long and significant history, still visible throughout this beautiful walk around Mirror Lake (#10 Pond) and Nelson Pond (Forest Lake). The area is a classic example of a small, rural nineteenth century mill village that processed local raw materials such as lumber, wool, and grain. It thrived as an industrial and commercial hub from 1812 to 1921, spanning the period from the construction of the first dam and sawmill, to the date when the War Memorial was placed at Memorial Hall.

Extensive laid-up stone foundations, bordering Pekin Brook and the outlet of Mirror Lake, represent the center of the village and give tribute to North Calais' industrious past. The dirt roads, surrounding the brook and marking the early part of the walk, are still lined with mid-nineteenth-century structures. They echo a time when North Calais was a bustling commercial hub on the stage route that ran from Montpelier to Hardwick and on to Newport and Canada. The hill road leading out of the village holds memories of the subsistence farmers who depended on the industry of the village to mill their wood, wool, cider, and grain.

Memorial Hall, built in 1886, is believed to be one of only two remaining GAR (Grand Army of the Republic) halls (the other is in Washington State). As you begin your walk, take time to stop at the lakeside memorial, a plaque giving tribute to the soldiers from Calais who died at war.

Walking the Loop:

Begin at GAR Road, which is an unmaintained road on the right side of the parking area. GAR Road skirts along the edge of Mirror Lake, passes Memorial Hall and ends up at the old mill site in the center of the

North Calais Loop

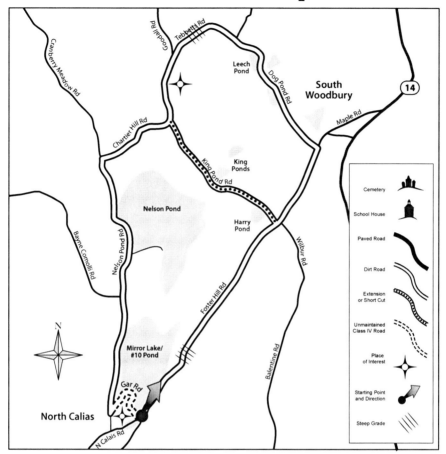

North Calais Loop—6.2 miles

* This loop can be shortened by turning left onto King Pond Road and cutting over to Chartier Hill Road *

- Park at public access for Mirror Lake/Number 10 Pond
- Walk along GAR Road. This is the small, unmaintained road that skirts along the water.
- Turn left onto North Calais Road
- Quickly veer left onto Foster Hill Road
- Turn left onto Dog Pond Road
- At fork, veer left onto Tebbetts Road
- At junction with King Pong Road, continue onto Chartier Hill Road
- Turn left onto Nelson Pond Road to skirt along Nelson and Mirror Lakes
- Reach junction with GAR Road

village. Take a left on North Calais Road and spend a moment checking out the nineteenth-century buildings and stone foundations surrounding Pekin Brook.

Ascend Foster Hill Road. At the beginning of the climb fill your water bottle at the natural spring that runs from a spigot into a wooden barrel across from the first house on your right.

Climb steadily along stone walls and ancient maples to reach rocky pastureland and a large homestead along the ridge. Descend down into Woodbury, with sweeping views looking north and east. Pass by King Pond Road and make a left onto Dog Pond Road as you enter into Woodbury Village.

Dog Pond Road is flat and wide as you leave Woodbury until it sweeps around Leech Pond past a colorful house and outbuildings covered with eccentric memorabilia. Stay left at the fork to continue on Tebetts Road. Climb up a very steep but beautiful section leading to Ezekial Ball Farm, settled in 1800. Walk under the "high drive" section of the barn and curve up and around the well-maintained farmhouse and adjoining property.

Walk along the ridge, with beautiful views to your left, and descend to the junction with King Pond Road. Continue straight onto Chartier Hill Road, walking downhill to reach a delightful crossroads. Make a left on Nelson Pond Road and follow the sounds of water to the banks of Nelson Pond (also called Forest Lake), the small and secluded neighbor of Mirror Lake. Skirt along the shore past seasonal camps and climb to the junction with Bayne Commoli Road. Continue straight past the junction to finish the loop with an easy stroll along the western side of Mirror Lake.

Section 4: Middlesex

Middlesex is a maze of funky folks and back roads lying hidden under the shadow of the Worcester range. What I notice in Middlesex, more than the old homesteads and lofty barns of neighboring East Montpelier and Calais, are newer houses that seem to capture the personality of the next generation of Central Vermonters. Look deeper into the landscape, and you will find hobby farmers with large organic gardens and yards filled with an assortment of goats, sheep, chickens, and pigs. Artistically bent folks hide away in the Middlesex hills, furtively revealing their presence by colorfully trimmed houses, welded metal sculptures, yurt studios, and rock cairns.

Walk #13 Dumpling Hill

How to get there:
From Montpelier: Take Route 12 North toward Worcester. After about five miles, veer left up Shady Rill Road. Turn right on Macey Road and cross over the bridge.

This wonderful meander follows roads around the base of Dumpling Hill, which you can spot from all sides as you move around the loop. It is a friendly walk with dogs that will follow you down the road, bright-colored houses, and, of course, the Dumpling Hill mailbox. * When you visit, don't forget to stop, listen to things you don't hear anywhere else, and leave a note.

The walk starts out along Macey Road following Martins and Patterson Brooks. When you reach the junction with West Hill Road you might get lucky and spot the shaggy Scottish Highland cows that graze along the road as you head right. West Hill Road is dirt, but is a busier road since it is the back way into Worcester Village. Always walk toward

Middlesex Loop

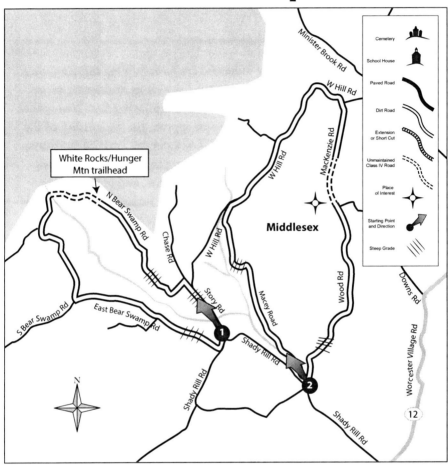

1. Bear Swamp Loop—5.4 miles

- Park near corner of Shady Hill and Story Road/West Hill Road
- Head up Story Road/ West Hill Road
- Fork left onto Chase Road
- Fork left onto North Bear Swamp Road

Sections of this road surrounding the trailhead are Class IV and unmaintained

- Turn left to continue down North Bear Swamp Road after the unmaintained stretch that passes by trailhead
- Stay left onto East Bear Swamp Road at the junction with its North and South Bear Swamp neighbors
- Turn left onto Shady Rill Road

traffic, and make sure you don't miss the turn up MacKenzie Road. It will be approximately 1.5 miles down West Hill on your right.

Follow the directions listed with the loop map to navigate the section of Class 4 Road, as MacKenzie transitions into the top of Wood Road. As the unmaintained section ends, you will see a yurt studio at the front of a well-maintained property on the right side of the road. Begin to look for the special Dumpling Hill mailbox at the top of Wood Road and enjoy this stretch of quiet country walking. Descend steadily down from the hill; notice the unique houses, gardens, and animals along the way. The last half-mile of Wood Road is very steep. One of my favorite things is to let gravity take over as I gallop, jog, or skip along this final stretch. Whooping is also fun. Be silly. Celebrate momentum. Breathe in the fresh air and take in the views of the Middlesex valley as you find your way back to Martins Brook.

A Moment on the Road

I was really confused the first time I completed the unmaintained section of this loop. At the edge of an abandoned property that seemed to be the solitary home of an ancient maple tree sat a light blue mailbox that read "Dumpling Hill". I know it's illegal to look through people's mail, but this mailbox was different. It begged to be opened and seemed like it belonged to the road itself. I peeked inside and found a little note-

---

2. Dumpling Hill—6.9 miles

- Park at the beginning of Macey Road after crossing over the bridge
- Head up Macey Road along brook
- Turn right onto West Hill Road
- Turn right onto MacKenzie Road *
- Continue straight onto Wood Road
- Reach junction with Macey Road

* *MacKenzie is a small, dead-end dirt road that is unmaintained at the end. Make sure you stay straight past the end of the houses as the view opens up. DO NOT follow the long driveway to the left, which leads toward the vista. As you follow MacKenzie Road (which is now a trail), the VAST snowmobile network intersects with the road. Stay straight until the road becomes maintained at the top of Wood Road.*

book with a woodcut print that read "sugaring", a red ribbon, and a pen. On the inside cover of the book I found a simple invitation:

A quiet place to stop and listen to the things we don't hear anywhere else. Have your picnic, walk a bit, and leave it clean for others. Leave us a note …

I flipped through the book, which was filled with the stray thoughts of walkers enjoying the solitude of the road and the serenity of time passing slowly. I found notes dated almost two years apart from a couple of very different walkers:

09/02/07—I am Hunter. I like Worcester. The school is great. I have lots of friends. I am in second grade.

09/07/09—Lovely summer into fall evening, walking with my dog. Twilight—Kimberly

Another time I found a flyer announcing a "Welcome Potluck" for the new families on Wood Road. The address of the event was listed, but the main instructions simply noted that the potluck was across from the "house with the green chimneys". These were obviously people who noticed the road and what surrounded them.

Walk #14 Bear Swamp

How to get there:

From Montpelier: Take Route 12 North toward Worcester. After about five miles, take a slight left up Shady Rill Road. After passing Rumney Memorial School, Storey Road will be on the right.

This wooded loop climbs steadily to the base of Mount Hunger and includes an unmaintained section that is best walked with snowshoes during times of deep snow. Start from the junction of Story Road and Shady Rill. Be sure to stay left, both when the road forks at West Hill Road/ Chase Road and then again at the junction of North Bear Swamp and Chase Road. There should be a homemade trail sign leading hikers to the Mount Hunger trailhead, letting you know you're heading in the right direction.

It might seem like the steady incline will never end, but your efforts will be rewarded at the top! At a strong bend in the road the views open, and a large property sits in a beautiful valley under the mountain ridge. Take time to notice the magnificent stonework and catch your breath after a long climb. This curve in the road marks the beginning of the un-maintained, isolated, and wild section of North Bear Swamp Road. Make sure you fork left as you make your way through this wonderful section of road so as not to end up on the access trail leading up to White Rocks/ Hunger Mountain.

When the Class IV section transitions back to road, turn left to continue down the maintained section of North Bear Swamp Road. Make sure to stay left on East Bear Swamp Road at the junction with its South Bear Swamp Road neighbor. Enjoy the wooded descent back toward Shady Rill. Be sure to give a friendly wave to other back-road travelers you might meet along the way.

Section 5: Northfield

Many people associate Northfield with Norwich University, America's first private military college. Though half the population of this small town lives in and around the village center, Northfield stretches all the way up to the base of the Northfield Ridge with many remote dirt roads, covered bridges, and babbling brooks. I have included two walking loops in this section that will take you into the more rural areas of Northfield. At the end of the loop descriptions, read the story of the "Pigman", one of the more infamous Vermont monsters, who has been spotted among the back roads of this area. Nervous that I might encounter the notorious Pigman on my journey into the hills, I was relieved to know there have been no sightings in over a decade. Maybe he has since retired.

 ## Stony Brook Loop

How to get there:
From Northfield: Take Route 12 South past Norwich University. Make a right onto Route 12 A. Turn right onto Stony Brook Road.

This is a great walk for beginners, with a flat, shady stroll along Stony Brook and some climbing along Smith Hill. There are small sections of paved road at the lower ends of Smith Hill and Stony Brook Roads. Your jaunt along Stony Brook Road will include the feathery shade of coniferous trees, a covered bridge, and the sound of rushing water hitting rocky shore. Smith Hill is a lovely road with a rolling landscape, hilltop views, and a steep but enjoyable descent at the end of the walk.

Northfield Stony Brook Loop

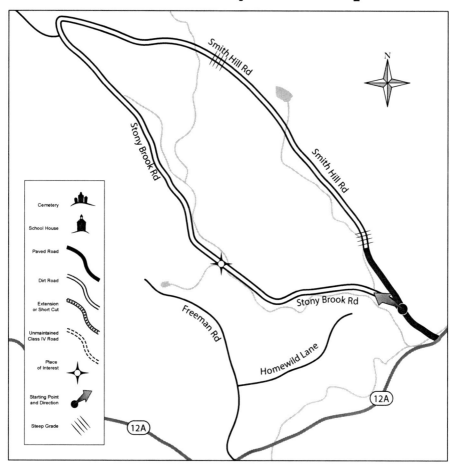

Northfield Stony Brook Loop—3.5 miles

- Park at bottom of Stony Brook Road
- Veer left onto Stony Brook Road at junction with Smith Hill Road
- Turn right onto Smith Hill Road
- Arrive back at junction with Stony Brook Road

Walk #16 Upper Northfield Loop

How to get there:

From Northfield: Take Route 12 South through Northfield Village. Turn right on 12 A. Make a right on Little Northfield Road. After approximately two miles, take a right on Gib Lane.

This is a gorgeous, very remote walk taking you right up against the underbelly of the Northfield Ridge. Highlights to notice along each road of the loop are:

Gib Lane:

- The property directly after Morning Star Lane is the Trijang Buddhist Institute. It is run by Trijang Rimpoche, said to be eighteenth in a line of eminent Indian and Tibetan masters. The hill property is beautiful with open fields separated by tidy stone walls.
- A historic farmhouse and outbuilding borders the road at the beginning of your journey. Both rest on immaculate dry stack stone foundations.
- Field Stone Farm is near the junction with Stony Brook Road. It is a gorgeous CSA farm offering organic vegetables, eggs, poultry, maple syrup, wood-fired flatbread, and homemade jellies and salsas. Check out the website: **http://fieldstonefarmvt.com/**

Stony Brook Road:

- Climb to the sound of the brook. Head up to a remote back-road junction with a renovated house built in 1807 and a huge stone foundation that is probably the footprint of a large outbuilding or barn.

(Pearl) Clark Road:

- A remote, wooded road, which hugs the base of the Northfield Ridge.
- This road levels off after an initial climb as ancient maples blend with a new generation of roadside hardwoods.

Upper Northfield Loop

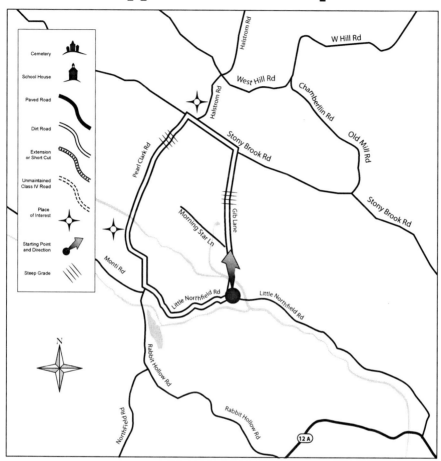

Upper Northfield Loop—3.4 miles

- Park near junction of Little Northfield Road and Gib Lane
- Walk up Gib Lane toward Morning Star Lane
- Turn left onto Stony Brook Road
- After passing Hallstrom Road on the right, take first left onto Pearl Clark Road
- Turn left onto Little Northfield Road
- Reach junction with Gib Lane

- After the brook crosses under the road, notice the beautiful old barn tucked up on the hillside to your right as the road curves to the left.

Old Northfield Road:
- The marshy section between Clark Road and Felchner Brook
- A large, sprawling property, speckled with various makeshift shelters, all seemingly in a permanent state of evolution: plastic, flapping insulation, plywood shacks built onto old trailers with wood smoke coming out of rickety stove pipes. It seems like a true collaboration of multiple households living free and independent up against the mountain.

Here is a simple version of the Pigman monster tale I found posted on http://newenglandfolkloreblogspot.com by Peter Muise on May 15, 2011. You may read more about the Pigman in books by Vermont author Joseph Citro, particularly *Weird New England* and *Green Mountains, Dark Tales*.

●

The Pigman of Northfield, Vermont

The time? 1971.

The place? A high school dance in picturesque Northfield, Vermont.

I'm sure you can imagine the scene. Crepe paper streamers, teens dancing to Led Zeppelin's "Stairway to Heaven," bell-bottom jeans, mediocre orange punch. A scene of small-town serenity.

However, small towns often have weird secrets, and Northfield's most shocking secret came to light that night when a group of students ran into the dance. They looked scared, and some of them were in tears.

They had been drinking beer in a sandpit behind the school, they said, when something strange came out of the woods. It was tall, naked, and covered in white hair. And although it walked on two legs, it had the face of a pig.

Whatever it was, it scared the hell out of the teens—they even abandoned the beer in their panic! Some of the braver students ventured out of the dance to investigate the sandpit. They didn't see the monster, but they did find the grass and underbrush had been trampled down. Something had been there. And thus the Pigman appeared in Northfield.

After the dance was disrupted, the locals made some strange connections. A farmer said he had seen a hideous naked figure rummaging through his trash a few nights earlier. More eerily, people remembered how a teenage boy disappeared from his family's farm six months ago. At the time authorities thought he had run away, but now people wondered if something more sinister had happened. Could he have been transformed into this strange monster? Or perhaps been eaten by it for dinner? A monster had to eat, and an awful lot of animals had gone missing recently …

The Pigman was seen in Northfield off and on for years, often around an area called the Devil's Washbowl. Motorists saw him run across the road, and teens who went to make out in the Washbowl sometimes had a surprise guest disrupt their romantic interlude.

Although the creature himself was somewhat elusive, physical evidence suggested he was real. A local man named Jeff Hatch and his friends found some caves near the Washbowl filled with animal bones and found a similar stash of gnawed bones in the town's only pig farm. Strange cloven footprints were also found in the soft ground.

I don't know if we'll ever know who (or what) the Pigman is. The top two theories are that the missing teenage boy somehow devolved and became feral or that some lonely farmer and a particularly friendly pig … well, you know what I mean. I don't think genetics work that way, but try telling that to the teens in Northfield, who still get spooked at night when they go drinking out in the woods.

Section 6: Plainfield Village and Beyond

People have come to Plainfield and its surrounding hills for centuries to find rest, inspiration, and self-sufficiency. In the late 1700's, early settlers arrived from New Hampshire, created pitches to designate boundary lines, and began the challenging task of carving out a life based around subsistence farming. In the latter part of the nineteenth century Plainfield was a popular summer resort town. Tourists would come from out of state to seek the healing spring waters found outside the village.

The railroad also arrived in the 1870s, bringing a boost to the tourist and commercial industry. Because the railroad could easily transport raw materials to and from the rural countryside, the village went through a period of economic prosperity as the focus moved from subsistence farming to industry. In its prime, Plainfield Village was filled with guesthouses, a clothes mill, sawmill, gristmill, and tannery, as well as factories producing wagons, sleighs, and carriages.

While the rail line stopped operating in 1956, the end of the twentieth century brought another generation of inspiration-seeking folks to the Plainfield area. By 1970, Goddard College became known as a radical institution and an epicenter for the counterculture movement. Self-directed students and free spirits came from all over the country to experiment with natural building methods, social justice, and creative ways of learning and living.

As you walk the loops up into the hills surrounding Plainfield Village, there is a sense of all this history weaving together. The sturdy farmhouses built as part of the original hill farms still stand next to the funky, creative structures of ex-Goddard students exploring innovative ways to live on the land.

If you are starting from the village, take time to check out the progressive food co-op and community center, homebrew store, art galleries, and used bookstore. If you want a treat, stop by Positive Pie on Main Street to indulge in a delicious brunch, handcrafted pizza, or a hoppy beer. Check out the website http://www.positivepie.com/ for more information and an updated menu. No matter which loop you choose,

Plainfield will inspire you with its hilly and lush landscape, funkiness, spacious views, and laid-back sensibility.

 **Plainfield Village Loop**

How to get there:

From Montpelier: Follow Route 2 East for approximately ten miles into Plainfield. Take a slight right down the hill to enter into the village on Main Street.

This walk starts in the village and ascends into the hills along rocky farmland with beautiful views looking back down into the valley. It begins and ends with sections of paved road. This is a great entry-level walk with one manageable climb and wide-open roads.

Plainfield Village Loop

Plainfield Village Loop—2.9 miles

- Park off of Main Street at the Plainfield Co-op
- Turn left onto Main Street
- Take the first right onto Creamery Street
- Turn left onto Brook Road
- Fork right onto Upper Road
- Take first right onto Center School Road
- Turn right onto Middle Road
- Continue onto Barre Hill
- Continue onto Mill Street
- Turn right onto Main Street to return to Plainfield Co-op

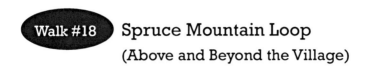

Walk #18 Spruce Mountain Loop
(Above and Beyond the Village)

How to get there:

From Plainfield Village: Head down Main Street and make a right on Creamery Road. Turn left onto Brook Road. Follow approximately 2.4 miles to the junction with Gray Road.

This varied loop takes you along Plainfield's Great Brook, climbs steeply up the backside of East Hill, and then gracefully descends along Gray Road. It will take you through rural life on Plainfield's back roads and provide ongoing views of the surrounding hillsides.

Note: If you enjoy your visit to Plainfield, you should consider a detour up Spruce Mountain (Spruce Mountain Road is off of East Hill between Brook Road and Gray Road). There is a beautiful 4.4-mile round-trip hike that takes you up to a fire tower offering 360-degree panoramic views. For more information about the hike up Spruce Mountain check out: **http://centralvermonthikes.blogspot.com/2010/05/spruce-mountain-plainfield-vermont.html**

Spruce Mountain Loop

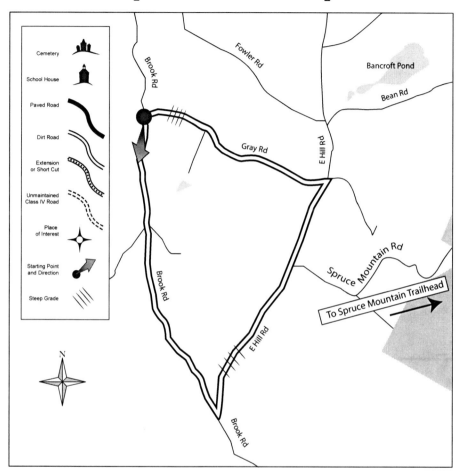

Spruce Mountain Loop (Plainfield)—3.7 miles

- Park near corner of Brook Road and Gray Road
- Head away from Plainfield Village (south) on Brook Road
- Make sharp left and ascend up East Hill Road
- Turn left onto Gray Road
- Reach junction of Gray Road and Brook Road

Section 7: Marshfield

Running along the border of Marshfield and Calais, these walks explore the rolling hillside between Route 14 and Route 2. Complete with varied terrain, views, old barns, and shady woods, these loops are gems on the northeast side of Washington County.

 **East Hill South**

How to get there:

From Montpelier: Follow Route 2 East to Route 14. Turn left on Route 14 North and proceed into East Calais. Take a sharp right on Marshfield Road before reaching East Calais General Store. Follow Marshfield Road for approximately 1.3 miles to reach the junction with East Hill Road.

Begin by heading south on East Hill past old, working farms with ongoing views of the Worcester Range looking west across rural Calais and Middlesex. Say good-bye to the open views of East Hill Road as you turn left on Sadie Foss Road. Make a quick, wooded ascent up to the junction with Hollister Hill. Head left on Hollister Hill. Ascend and descend through undulating terrain as you wind through woods and past delightful views east toward Marshfield. Make a left onto the Calais/Marshfield Road, step over the town line into Calais, and head west along this shady stretch back to your car.

East Hill North

How to get there:

From Montpelier: Follow Route 2 East to Route 14. Turn left onto Route 14 North and take into East Calais. Take sharp right on Marshfield Road before reaching East Calais General Store. Follow Marshfield Road for approximately 1.3 miles to reach the junction with East Hill Road.

Walking the Loop:

- Park at the corner of East Hill Road.
- Head down the Marshfield/Calais Road using this shady, flat section as a way to warm up to the walk. Listen to your footsteps, notice your breath, and let your mind take its time to empty.
- Turn left onto Hollister Hill, where the road will dead-end at a brick farmhouse built in 1835 surrounded by extensive gardens, a small orchard, and secluded serenity. The road turns into a steep trail, which is also used for logging. Walk up and over the hillside past an old sugarhouse, camping hut, and long line of ancient maples still tapped for their delicious spring sugar.
- The trail will turn into Al Ennis Place to take you to the junction of May Road and Ennis Hill Road.
- Head slight left onto Ennis Hill Road, which follows the ridgeline past an old working farm with extensive hayfields and woodlots. Take in the views to the east and south. Note: While three big dogs (who will bark and seem scary) live on this property, they are friendly to both people and other dogs.
- Turn left onto Blachly/East Hill Road and cross over the town line into Calais. Climb steeply up and over the hillside to pass by Unadilla Theatre (Broadview Farm) at the top of East Hill.
- Make a brief, wooded descent to the junction with Bliss Road and the entrance to the Roots Wilderness School, which will be on your left.
- Complete the walk with a hilly finish past the Bohemia Bakery on

Marshfield Loops

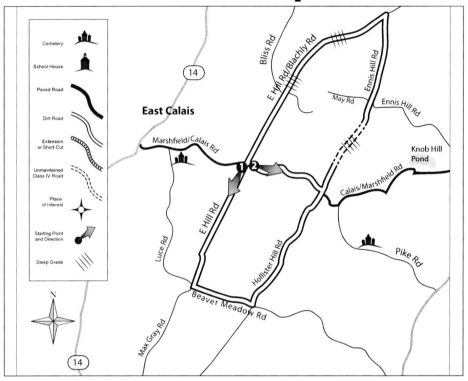

1. East Hill South (Marshfield)—4.3 miles
- Park near corner of Marshfield/Calais Road and East Hill Road
- Head south onto East Hill Road toward Luce Road
- Turn left onto Beaver Meadow Road
- Take first left onto Hollister Hill Road
- Turn left onto Calais/Marshfield Road
- Arrive back at junction with East Hill Road

2. East Hill North (Marshfield)—4.9 miles
- Park near corner of East Hill Road and head east on Marshfield/Calais Road
- Turn left onto Hollister Hill Road
- Follow maintained section of road past brick farmhouse, and head straight onto trail (Steep class IV section)
- Follow trail over hillside and continue to junction with May Road and Ennis Hill Road
- Veer slightly left onto Ennis Hill Road
- Turn left onto East Hill Road/ Blachly Road
- Continue past junction with Bliss Road
- Arrive at junction with Marshfield/Calais Road

your left before reaching the junction with the main road between Calais and Marshfield.

A Moment on the Road

I discovered this beautiful walk after getting stuck in a ditch on the corner of East Hill and Ennis Hill Road. I was coming from the Manifestivus Music Festival in Cabot, and the winding rural roads had caused me to lose my bearings. I went to turn around next to an old house with a dilapidated barn and overgrown flower garden, missed the gravel driveway by a few inches, and backed up right into a ditch. I had no choice but to knock on the door and ask for help.

Dogs started barking, cats came out from hiding and ran under the porch, and an elderly lady answered the door. She had white hair in braids and a sparkle in her eye. We talked about weaving and how she and her late husband moved to Vermont many years ago to get away from the hustle and bustle of New York City. She seemed to know just about everyone in the area and phoned the young man farther up Ennis Hill Road, who lived on a property owned by an older farmer. He helped maintain the land by haying the fields and logging the woodlots.

This country gentleman came right away with his truck and some chains, and effortlessly pulled my car out of the ditch. We proceeded to have a charming chat on the backside of his truck over a couple of hand-rolled cigarettes.

While waiting for him to arrive, I sat looking over the ridge and studying my map. I was delighted to notice that the surrounding roads circled through the hilly countryside. I decided after such an enchanting rescue that I would come back and explore the loop.

This loop has never ceased to inspire me. It takes the walker along a mysterious unmaintained section of road, up along an open ridgeline, and past Unadilla Theatre and Roots Wilderness Survival School **(http://www.rootsvt.com/)**. If you walk in late March, right before the beginning of mud season, you might even have the pleasure of catching a herd of young lambs and their mothers enjoying fresh hay and the cool, spring air on the top of East Hill.

Section 8: Last But Not Least

 **Cabot**

How to get there:

From Montpelier: Follow Route 2 East into Marshfield. Turn left on Route 215/Cabot Road. Turn left onto West Hill Pond Road to reach the junction with Coits Pond Road.

Situated in the northeast corner of Washington County on the border of the Northeast Kingdom, Cabot is an agricultural community of twelve hundred people, and is home of the Cabot Creamery. This spectacular stroll takes you through the high, pastoral valley of Cabot. It meanders past large, picturesque dairy farms framed within ongoing and extensive views of the Northeast Kingdom's patchwork landscape.

Start at West Hill Pond and climb steeply above Cabot Village along Coits Pond Road. Notice the gnarled sugar maples along the side of the road, and see if you can spot any old tap holes as you peer closer into the split bark. The road levels out just before the junction with Churchill

Cabot Loop

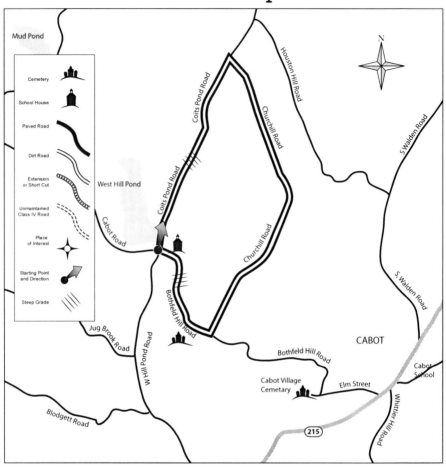

Cabot Loop—3.7 miles

- Park at West Hill Pond
- Walk up Coits Pond Road
- Turn right onto Churchill Road
- Turn right onto Bothfeld Hill Road
- Arrive back at West Hill Pond and junction with Coits Pond Road

Road as the view and landscape dramatically shift.

Make a right on Churchill Road, walking directly across the ridge above the valley. The walk stays level and the views look out toward the Northeast Kingdom. The road weaves through the dairy farms of Cabot and their surrounding fields and woodlots.

It is obvious that Cabot has been an agricultural community for hundreds of years, because of the way the old farms, open fields, woods, stone walls, distant mountains, and even the smell of cow manure feel like integral parts of the working landscape. It seems that the weathered farmers driving through the mud on their tractors have withstood the test of time. They stoically persist season after season doing what their ancestors have always done.

Make a right at the Bothfeld Farm onto Bothfeld Hill Road. Pass the West Hill Cemetery on your left and make a brief, wooded descent back toward the road junction and the beginning of the walk. Take time at the bottom of the hill to notice the restored West Hill Schoolhouse (circa 1853–1918) on your right before reaching the pond and the end of the loop.

How to get there:

From Interstate 89: Take Exit 7 and merge onto VT 62 East. At the first traffic light, make a right onto Paine Turnpike North. Take the next right onto Crosstown Road. Turn left onto Paine Turnpike South. The next junction is Brookfield Road.

If you want your walk to be less solitary and welcome the camaraderie of other walkers, Berlin Pond is the place to be. This is probably the most popular of all the walks in this book. The relatively flat terrain, easy parking access, and beautiful scenery lend themselves to walkers of all ages and fitness levels. While the interstate runs parallel to the last half mile of the Paine Turnpike, this loop is still known as a recreational gem in Washington County.

The pond is also part of the Vermont Audubon Society's preservation

Berlin Pond Loop

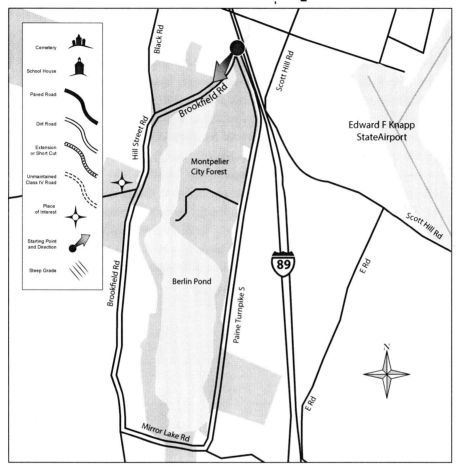

Berlin Pond Loop—5.0 miles

- Park in the parking area designated for recreational users on Brookfield Road
- Walk up (southwest) Brookfield Road toward Black Road/Hill Street Road
- Turn left onto Mirror Lake Road
- Take the first left onto Paine Turnpike South
- Turn left onto Brookfield Road to reach parking area

efforts and is designated as part of the Important Bird Area Program. Birders frequent the more remote areas of the walk in search of species such as the common loon, pied-billed Grebe, sora, and goshawk.

I don't usually go into too much detail about trailheads near or on these loop walks since my intention is to focus mostly on road walking. The Irish Hill Recreational Area's focal point, however, is an antique road leading up to an old homestead site, so it seems appropriate to include a few side notes about this multiuse trail system.

About a mile from the beginning of Brookfield Road is a parking area on the right for the Irish Hill Recreational Area frequented by hikers, mountain bikers, and motorized recreational vehicles. The Darling Road Trail will take you up past the site of the Steward Homestead, one of the first frame houses constructed in Berlin and continuously occupied by six generations of the Stewart family until the late 1940s. There is a ridgeline trail off of the old road that leads to a nice vista overlooking the pond. For a side adventure, you can easily access maps of this recreational area on http://www.berlinvt.org.

Waterbury Center

How to get there:

From Waterbury: Take Route 100 North toward Stowe. After passing the Ben & Jerry's factory, turn right on Guptil Road. Take a right onto Kneeland Flats Road. Reach the junction with Shaw Mansion Road.

This is a moderate walk peppered with unexpected lawn art, beautiful views, and good hill walking. While this stroll does not have as many historic barns or homesteads as some of the other walks in Washington County, it is close to the Worcester range and has beautiful views of Camel's Hump and its surrounding ridgeline. Loomis Hill Cemetery is also worth a visit on your way around the loop. It is located between Ripley and Shaw Mansion Road, tucked off the left side of Loomis Hill Road.

The walk stays mostly on dirt roads, although there are short areas of paved road at the beginning of Ripley Road and at the top of the climb on Loomis Hill Road. If you want a sweet to compliment your walk, I suggest taking a short detour into Waterbury Center for a visit to Cold

Waterbury Center/ Loomis Hill Loop

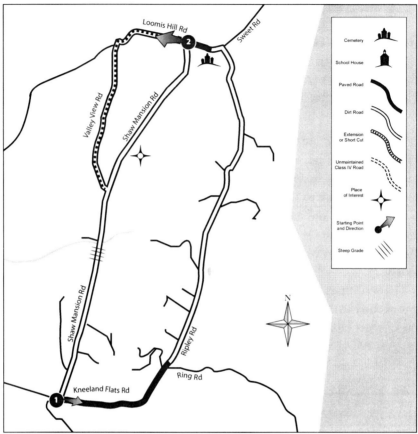

**Waterbury Center/ Loomis Hill Loop—4.6 miles
with Valley View Extension—5.2 miles**

1. Loomis Hill Loop

- Park near corner of Kneeland Flats Road and Shaw Mansion Road
- Head up Kneeland Flats Road and continue straight onto Ripley Road
- Turn left onto Loomis Hill Road
- Turn left onto Shaw Mansion Road
- Arrive back at junction with Kneeland Flats Road

2. With Valley View Extension

- Head up Kneeland Flats Road
- Continue straight onto Ripley Road
- Turn left onto Loomis Hill Road
- Turn left onto Valley View Road
- Turn right onto Shaw Mansion Road

Hollow Cider Mill for an iconic cider donut or other Vermont treats. If you prefer a creamy indulgence, this walk is minutes away from the Ben & Jerry's factory.

Here are some not-to-be-missed highlights:
- Old barn with the curved roof at Severence Farm near the top of Shaw Mansion Road
- Loomis Hill Cemetery
- View at the top of Loomis Hill (best seen at the junction of Valley View and Loomis Hill)
- The funky chicken co-op near the bottom of Shaw Mansion Road

Invitation

This book is about exploration and inquiry. Let these walks encourage you to wonder as you wander. Let the road transform you but always lead you back to the place where you are …

- Back to the rhythm of your breath, heartbeat, and footsteps
- Back to the story of a landscape shaped by the hard work of independent, free-spirited people
- Back to the sheer joy of having nothing else to do but be
- Back to a time when people waved as they passed and men in muddy pickup trucks pulled over to see if you needed a hand
- Back to the sound of cattails rustling over rippling marshes
- Back to the lengthened shadows of dusk
- Back to the wet noses of calves chewing hay in verdant valleys
- Circling back, back, and back again to this fleeting, extended moment of walking along the open road

Fair Warning …
- Flat is not often part of the Vermont landscape.
- If you want straight, take the highway.
- The moment will change you.

Remember that not all who wander are lost.
Enjoy the journey.

The end ....

or the beginning ...

Walking man walk. Walk on by my door. Well, any other man stops and talks but not the walking man. He's the walking man, born to walk, walk on walking man.

Well now, would he have wings to fly? Would he be free? Golden wings against the sky, walking man, walk on by. So long, walking man.

— James Taylor

Resources

Want to Wander More Deeply into the Road's Past?

Historical Societies (http://www.vermonthistory.org/index.php/
local-history/local-societies-directory/washington-county.html)

Cabot Historical Society
West Hill School House, West Hill 4 Corners, Cabot, Vermont
Mailing Address: PO Box 275, Cabot, VT 05647
Website: www.cabothistory.com
E-mail: bonniesd@together.net
Phone: (802) 563-3396
Contact: Bonnie Dannenberg, president
The society has restored a one-room schoolhouse, as well as another
school that was used as a Good Templars' hall. Collections include
household furnishings, medical practice materials, tools and farming
implements, documents from 1800 to 1920, photographs, and turn-of-
the-twentieth-century educational materials. Visitors by appointment.
The Main Street Museum will be open on the second Saturday of each
month from 1:00 p.m. to 3:00 p.m., from June through early Septem-
ber. Also open by appointment.

Calais Historical Society
Mailing Address: PO Box 8, Adamant, VT 05640
Contact Person: Peter Harvey, president
Visitors by appointment.

East Montpelier Historical Society
Town Office, East Montpelier Village, Vermont
Mailing Address: PO Box 63, East Montpelier, VT 05651
Website: www.eastmontpelierhistoricalsociety.org/index.html
E-mail: dave.coburn@comcast.net

Phone: (802) 223–6886

Contact: David Coburn

The society does not have a physical location, but its collection includes the town history *Across the Onion*, and publications *Revolutionary War Soldiers and Cemeteries of East Montpelier*, all of which are available at the town office in East Montpelier village. The society also has a collection of photographs of buildings and life in town.

Hours and Admission: town office hours by appointment

Fayston Historical Society

Mailing Address: 3685 North Fayston Road, Moretown, VT 05660

Phone: (802) 496–2083

Contact: Nicolle Migneault, rmigneault@aol.com

Hours and Admission: May 1 through December 1: by appointment

Marshfield Historical Society

Town Hall, 122 School Street, Marshfield, Vermont

Mailing Address: 5378 Hollister Hill Road, Marshfield, VT 05658

E-mail: jpjhistory@netscape.net

Phone: (802) 426–3411

Contact: John Johnson, president

The society has exhibits of local history in the town hall. Visitors by appointment.

Middlesex Historical Society

5 Church Street, Middlesex, Vermont

Mailing Address: 5 Church Street, Middlesex, VT 05602

Website: http://www.middlesex-vt.org/html/historical_society.html

E-mail: pwiley3@gmail.com

Phone: (802) 272–8074

Contact: Patricia Wiley, president

The society was founded in 1993 and does not yet have a permanent home. In 2006 the society published the first comprehensive written history of the town of Middlesex. Ongoing projects include collecting oral history, photographs, and other items for future display. Visitors by appointment.

Moretown Historical Society

Memorial Library, Moretown, Vermont
Mailing Address: 800 South Hill Road, Moretown, VT 05660
Website: www.moretownvt.com/history3.html
E-mail: dgabaree@hotmail.com
Phone: (802) 496–2090
Contact: Denise Gabaree, president
The society is located at the Moretown Memorial Library and is in the process of renovating the building. Meetings are the third Wednesday of each month at 7:30 p.m. at the library.
Visitors by appointment. Free.

Northfield Historical Society

Governor Charles Paine House, 75 South Main Street, North-field, Vermont
Mailing Address: PO Box 422, Northfield, VT 05663
Website: www.sites.google.com/site/northfieldvthistoricalsociety/
E-mail: nhscurator@trans-video.net
Phone: (802) 485–4792, Charles Paine House
Contact: Barbara Pope bbpope@tds.net
Hours and Admission: Open by appointment. Admission is free but donations are graciously accepted.

Plainfield Historical Society

Cutler Memorial Library, High Street, US Route 2, Plainfield, Vermont
Mailing Address: PO Box 223, Plainfield, VT 05667
Phone: (802) 454–1418
Contact: David Strong, president
Hours and Admission: by appointment

Waitsfield Historical Society

General Benjamin Wait House, VT Route 100, Waitsfield, Vermont
Mailing Address: PO Box 816, Waitsfield, VT 05673

Website: www.waitsfieldhistoricalsociety.com
E-mail: JEMD@WCVT.com
Phone: (802) 496–2027
Contact: Judy Dodds, curator

The society's home originally belonged to General Benjamin Wait and was moved to its present location in 1830. It was renovated in 1997. The society has offices upstairs and maintains historical exhibits in the downstairs room. The exhibits are changed periodically and are open to the public when the Wait House is open. The society specializes in oral histories, military artifacts, research materials, genealogies, and photographs (mostly from 1870 to 1920).

Hours and Admission: Monday-Friday, 10:00 a.m. to 5:00 p.m.; Saturday, 10:00 a.m. to noon.

Waterbury Historical Society

Museum, Waterbury Public Library, 28 North Main Street, Waterbury, Vermont
Mailing Address: PO Box 708, Waterbury, VT 05676
Website: http://www.rootsweb.com/~vtwhs/
E-mail: waterburyhistoricalsociety@hotmail.com
Phone: (802) 244–7067
Contact: Brian Lindner, president, (802) 229–3880, BLindner@ nationallife.com

The museum displays its collections of Civil War memorabilia and articles relating to the history of the area in rooms located above the town library. The building is the former home of Civil War surgeon Dr. Henry Janes.

Hours and Admission: Library hours or by appointment

CPSIA information can be obtained at www.ICGtesting.com
Printed in the USA
BVOW03s1534271013

334701BV00006B/142/P